The taste of Fitness

Helen O'Connor
and Donna Hay

J B F P

EDITORIAL
Food Editor: Rachel Blackmore
Subeditors: Ella Martin, Katrina O'Brien
Editorial and Production Assistant: Allison Ellul
Editorial Coordinator: Margaret Kelly

PHOTOGRAPHY
Quentin Bacon

DESIGN AND PRODUCTION
Managers: Sheridan Carter, Anna Maguire
Layout and Design: Gavin Murrell
Production Artist: Lulu Dougherty
Production Editor and Cover Design: Sheridan Packer

ACKNOWLEDGMENTS
The authors and publisher wish to thank the following people
for their support and assistance with this book.
Consultant Dietitians: Maureen O'Connor, Soumella Amanatidis
and Sue Munro for editoral comments.
Brad Childs for his continual support and many hours of
typing.

Published by J.B. Fairfax Press Pty Limited
80-82 McLachlan Avenue
Rushcutters Bay, NSW 2011, Australia
A.C.N. 003 738 430

Formatted by J.B. Fairfax Press Pty Limited
Printed by Toppan Printing Co, Singapore
PRINTED IN SINGAPORE

This book is a revised and expanded edition of *The Taste of
Fitness* published in 1993.

JBFP 425
Includes Index
ISBN 1 86343 255 8

DISTRIBUTION AND SALES
All enquiries: J.B. Fairfax Press Pty Limited
Ph: (02) 9361 6366 Fax: (02) 9360 6262
http://www.jbfp.com.au

About this Book

Nutritional analysis

Each recipe has been computer
analysed for its kilojoule (calorie),
fat and carbohydrate content. Based
on the amount of fat and the
percentage of energy from
carbohydrate, the recipes have
been rated according to the
following guidelines:

Carbohydrate

Rated on the percentage of energy
(kilojoules/calories) from
carbohydrate:

less than 50%	*low*
50-55%	*medium*
56-69%	*high*
70% or more	*very high*

Fat

Rated on the grams of fat per
serving:

less than 5 g	*very low*
5 g to less than 10 g	*low*
10-15 g	*medium*
more than 15 g	*high*

The pantry shelf

Unless otherwise stated, the
following ingredients used in this
book are:

Flour – White flour, plain or standard

Sugar – White sugar

What's in a tablespoon?

Australia:
  *1 tablespoon = 20 mL or
  4 teaspoons*
New Zealand:
  *1 tablespoon = 15 mL or
  3 teaspoons*
United Kingdom:
  *1 tablespoon = 15 mL or
  3 teaspoons*

The recipes in this book were
tested in Australia where a
20 mL tablespoon is standard.
All measures are level.
  The tablespoon in the New
Zealand and United Kingdom sets of
measuring spoons is 15 mL. In
many recipes this difference will not
matter. For recipes using baking
powder, gelatine, bicarbonate of
soda, and small quantities of flour
and cornflour, simply add another
teaspoon for each tablespoon
specified.

CONTENTS

A BALANCED DIET
THE KEY TO SUCCESS

*Forget what you've heard about good and bad foods. Balanced
eating means that you can eat all foods – it's just that it's best if
you eat more of some than others. Is your diet well balanced?
Do this quiz and find out how well you score.*

NUTRITION CHECK LIST

		Yes	No
1	I eat at least 3-4 slices of bread a day. (1 roll = 2 slices of bread)	☐	☐
2	I eat one serve of breakfast cereal each day – or an extra slice of bread.	☐	☐
3	I eat at least one piece of fruit each day.	☐	☐
4	I mostly eat wholegrain breads and cereals.	☐	☐
5	I eat at least 3 vegetables or have a salad most days.	☐	☐
6	I eat at least 1 and usually 2 serves of meat or meat alternative (poultry, seafood, eggs or dried peas/beans, nuts) each day.	☐	☐
7	I spread butter or margarine thinly on bread or use none at all.	☐	☐
8	I fry no more than once a week.	☐	☐
9	I use only polyunsaturated or mono-unsaturated oil (canola or olive oil) for cooking. (Tick YES if you never fry in oil or fat.)	☐	☐
10	I avoid oil-based dressings on salads.	☐	☐
11	I use reduced-fat dairy products.	☐	☐
12	I cut the fat off meat and take the skin off chicken.	☐	☐
13	I drink no more than 4 cups of tea, coffee, hot chocolate, coke or caffeine-containing drinks each day.	☐	☐
14	I avoid adding salt to my food.	☐	☐
15	I eat fatty snacks such as chocolate, chips etc. no more than once a week.	☐	☐
16	I eat 3 serves of dairy food or soy milk alternative each day. 1 serve = 200 mL/6$\frac{1}{2}$ fl oz milk; 1 slice (30 g/1 oz) hard cheese; 200 g/6$\frac{1}{2}$ oz yogurt; or 200 mL/6$\frac{1}{2}$ fl oz fortified soy milk.	☐	☐
17	I would skip a breakfast, lunch or dinner meal, no more than once a week.	☐	☐
18	I am aware of the best sources of iron and try to include an iron-rich food in my diet each day. (See page 41 for information on iron-rich foods.)	☐	☐
19	When I drink alcohol, I would mostly drink no more than 2 standard drinks (see page 34 for information on what is a standard drink) on any day and would rarely drink alcohol more than is recommended as the safe drink driving limit. (Tick YES if you don't drink alcohol.)	☐	☐
20	I eat fast/takeaway food no more than once a week.	☐	☐

TOTAL _____

Scoring: For each YES answer score 1 point.

18 or more	Excellent
15–17	Room for improvement
12–14	Just made it
less than 12	Poor

Very active people will need to eat more breads, cereals and fruit than indicated in this quiz, but to stay healthy no one should be eating less. Use this quiz as a personal nutrition check list or to rate a diet you may read in a book or magazine. It will help you to sort out the good diets from the fad diets.

The Winning Plate

The typical home-cooked meal may look wholesome, but the proportions of
nutrients eaten by most people in the Western world are unbalanced.
We eat too much fat and not enough complex carbohydrate or fibre.

TYPICAL PLATE

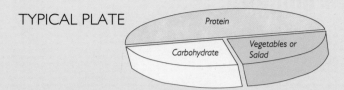

- Carbohydrate serve too small
- Fat often added to carbohydrate serve
e.g. fried chips, fried rice, excess butter on bread,
cream sauce on pasta
- Fibre content of meal not enough, sometimes
no vegetables or salad at all
- Vegetables often overcooked or cooked with
added fat
- Salads often served with an oil-based dressing
- Protein portion often cooked in fat
- Fatty meat, poultry with skin, or fried seafood
add more fat to the meal

WINNING PLATE

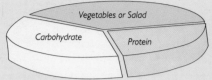

- High-carbohydrate and high-fibre foods,
such as bread, pasta, rice or potatoes,
make up 60-70% of the meal
- Choose lean meats
- Remove fat and skin from poultry
- Grill, steam, dry-fry or bake meat, poultry
and seafood. Avoid cooking in fat
- Generous serve of high-fibre foods, such as
vegetables or salads, prepared without fat

To maintain good health and improve physical performance, we need to turn
the tables on our current food habits and practices. We can make a start by
altering the proportions of food on our plate.

Plates Pillivuyt

BREAKFAST
FUELLING FOR THE DAY AHEAD

Banana Porridge

Serves 2

2 cups/500 mL/16 fl oz skim milk
2 cups/185 g/6 oz rolled oats
2 bananas, roughly chopped
1/2 teaspoon ground cinnamon (optional)

1   Place milk in a saucepan and heat, stirring occasionally, over a medium heat for 1-2 minutes or until hot.

2   Stir in rolled oats and cook, stirring constantly, for 2-3 minutes or until oats are soft. Add banana and mix to combine.

3   Spoon porridge into serving bowls, sprinkle with cinnamon and top with 3/4 cup/185 mL/6 fl oz skim milk.

Microwave it: Place milk in a microwave-safe container and cook on HIGH (100%) for 1 minute, stir in rolled oats and cook on HIGH (100%) for 1 minute longer. Stir in banana, sprinkle with cinnamon and serve.

1265 kilojoules (300 Calories) per serve		
Carbohydrate	52.5 g (69%)	high
Fat	4 g	very low

Apple and Sultana Porridge
Replace banana with 1 grated apple and 3 tablespoons sultanas.

1285 kilojoules (305 Calories) per serve		
Carbohydrate	55 g (70%)	very high
Fat	4 g	very low

Pear and Yogurt Porridge
Replace banana with 1 roughly chopped pear and instead of serving with milk, serve with 1/2 cup/ 125 g/4 oz low-fat natural, vanilla or fruit-flavoured yogurt.

1020 kilojoules (265 Calories) per serve		
Carbohydrate	43.5 g (64%)	high
Fat	4 g	very low

Fast Frittata

Serves 2

2 slices reduced-fat-and-salt ham, chopped
1/2 red pepper, sliced
1 tomato, chopped
1 small zucchini (courgette), cut into strips
2 eggs, lightly beaten
3/4 cup/185 mL/6 fl oz reduced-fat milk
1/2 teaspoon dried mixed herbs or
1 tablespoon chopped fresh herbs of your choice
freshly ground black pepper

1   Place ham, red pepper, tomato and zucchini (courgette) in a small nonstick frying pan and cook over a medium heat for 2-3 minutes or until vegetables are soft.

2   Place eggs, milk, herbs and black pepper to taste in a bowl and whisk to combine.

3   Pour egg mixture over vegetable mixture and cook over a low heat for 3-4 minutes or until frittata is set.

4   Place frittata under a preheated hot grill and cook for 1 minute or until top is browned. Serve hot with toast.

Lunchbox idea: Frittata is also delicious eaten cold. Allow to cool, then wrap in plastic food wrap. The frittata will keep in the refrigerator for up to 3 days.

615 kilojoules (145 Calories) per serve		
Carbohydrate	8 g (20%)	low
Fat	6 g	low

Magic Muesli

Serves 2

2 cups/250 g/8 oz untoasted muesli
4 cups/1 litre/1 3/4 pt skim milk or orange juice

Place muesli in a bowl, pour over milk or orange juice, cover and refrigerate overnight. Serve cold or heat and eat warm.

To heat: Place muesli mixture in a saucepan and cook, stirring, over a medium heat for 4-5 minutes or until heated through.

Microwave it: Remove cover from bowl and cook on HIGH (100%) for 4-5 minutes. Stir after 2 minutes. Remember to use a microwave-safe bowl.

1240 kilojoules (295 Calories) per serve with milk		
Carbohydrate	45 g (59%)	high
Fat	6 g	low

1230 kilojoules (293 Calories) per serve with juice		
Carbohydrate	51 g (69%)	high
Fat	6 g	low

Ham and Egg Pie

Serves 4
Oven temp: 180°C, 350°F, Gas 4

4 6 slices white or wholemeal bread, crusts removed
4 slices reduced-fat-and-salt ham, chopped
4 3 eggs, lightly beaten
3 1/4 teaspoon wholegrain mustard
1 1/4 1 1/2 cups/375 mL/12 fl oz reduced-fat milk
30 g/1 oz grated reduced-fat Cheddar cheese
1/2 tsp salt   pepper to taste

1   Line a 20 cm/8 in square cake tin with nonstick baking paper. Line base of tin with bread slices, cutting slices to fit.

2   Heat a nonstick frying pan, add ham and cook, stirring, for 3-4 minutes or until crisp. Remove ham from pan, drain on absorbent kitchen paper and sprinkle over bread.

3   Place eggs, mustard, milk and cheese in a bowl and whisk to combine. Pour egg mixture into tin and bake for 25-30 minutes or until puffed and golden.

Cook's tip: This makes a great hot breakfast or is just as delicious cold for lunch or snacks.

985 kilojoules (235 Calories) per serve		
Carbohydrate	22 g (37%)	low
Fat	8 g	low

add mushrooms + gr/red pepper

Magic Muesli, Banana Porridge, Ham and Egg Pie, Fast Frittata

The Importance of Breakfast

Breakfast is the meal which breaks the overnight fast, hence the name 'breakfast'.

Statistics worldwide show that breakfast is frequently skipped. For those of you who are tempted to skip breakfast, remember that nutrients missed at breakfast are seldom made up during the day. For active people, a good breakfast ensures that their bodies are fuelled and ready for physical activity.

The following are some of the most frequently asked questions about breakfast:

'Should I eat breakfast before or after training?'

It may be easier for early morning exercisers to eat breakfast after training. However, if you exercise strenuously for over an hour, it is best if you eat or drink something containing carbohydrate prior to training, even if it's only part of your full breakfast. Eat the rest of your breakfast after training to refuel your muscles for the day ahead. Sports drinks (see page 32), juices or reduced-fat milk drinks (page 31) are great if you find it difficult to train on a full stomach.

'I don't have time to eat breakfast in the morning. How can I catch up through the day?'

Firstly, a healthy breakfast can be fast. The recipes in this book are designed to be quick, easy to prepare as well as healthy. You only need to spend 5-10 minutes extra in the morning and for your body's sake it's worth it. If you can't manage food, try a liquid breakfast. You'll find some energising recipes in the drinks section (page 31). Have one of these drinks on the way to school or work or instead of that cup of coffee at morning tea.

Alternatively, take healthy snacks (page 11) or extra lunch (page 20) along with you so you can grab a quick bite of something healthy when you get a break through the morning.

'What should I eat for breakfast?'

The best foods to include are those which are high in carbohydrate and low in fat. Wholegrain breads and cereals, fruit and juice. Top cereal with reduced-fat milk or low-fat yogurt. Choosing a combination of these foods helps you obtain a range of nutrients. Best hot options include baked beans, spaghetti and pancakes. See recipe section for other ideas.

'I'm trying to lose weight. Should I eat breakfast?'

Many dieters skip breakfast. Research suggests that breakfast skippers are more often overweight! Skipping breakfast makes you hungrier at other times of the day – usually between meals when it's easy to snack on foods that are high in fat and sugar. A good breakfast will keep you going for hours and helps you to control cravings for sugary or fatty foods.

'Is there anything I should avoid at breakfast?'

Sausages, bacon, fried eggs, croissants, pastries and the like are high in fat and therefore best avoided. Whilst the occasional splurge is okay, aim to keep to the cereals, breads and fruit which provide carbohydrate and a minimum of fat.

'Should breakfast be the biggest meal of the day?'

The old expression, 'Breakfast like a king, lunch like a queen and dine like a pauper', reinforces the principle of eating substantially through the day when you are most active. If you are in heavy training, you may need three king-size meals plus snacks in between. A substantial evening meal is fine, provided you have eaten well throughout the day – don't save up a day's worth of food for just one evening meal. Eating well in the evening is vital for recovery if you train hard in the afternoon.

'How do I select the right breakfast cereal?'

Read the labels on cereal boxes. Compare the amount of fat, fibre and carbohydrate. Avoid toasted cereals – they are toasted in fat.

SPORTING SNACKS
TIME OUT TO TOP UP ON CARBOHYDRATE AND ENERGY

Banana Muffins

Makes 6 large muffins
Oven temp: 190°C, 375°F, Gas 5

2 cups/250 g/8 oz self-raising flour
¹/₂ cup/90 g/3 oz brown sugar
¹/₂ teaspoon ground cinnamon
3 bananas, mashed
1 egg, lightly beaten
1 cup/200 g/6¹/₂ oz lite vanilla *fromage frais*
¹/₂ cup/125 mL/4 fl oz reduced-fat milk or buttermilk

1   Place flour, sugar and cinnamon in a bowl and mix to combine. Add bananas, egg, *fromage frais* and milk and mix lightly. Take care not to overmix.

2   Spoon mixture into six nonstick large muffins tins and bake for 25-30 minutes or until cooked.

1240 kilojoules (295 Calories) per muffin
Carbohydrate	62 g (82%)	very high
Fat	1.7 g	very low

Apple and Cinnamon Muffins
Replace bananas with 1 cup/250 g/8 oz canned, unsweetened pie apple. Add an extra ¹/₂ teaspoon ground cinnamon and 2 teaspoons finely grated lemon rind.

1095 kilojoules (260 Calories) per muffin
Carbohydrate	54 g (81%)	very high
Fat	1.7 g	very low

Blueberry Muffins
Replace bananas with 125 g/4 oz fresh or frozen blueberries and add 2 teaspoons finely grated lemon rind.

1100 kilojoules (262 Calories) per muffin
Carbohydrate	54 g (81%)	very high
Fat	1.7 g	very low

Muesli Bars

Makes 14 bars
Oven temp: 180°C, 350°F, Gas 4

2 cups/185 g/6 oz rolled oats
6 Weet-Bix (Weetabix), lightly crushed
¹/₂ cup/90 g/3 oz raisins
60 g/2 oz chopped dried apricots
¹/₂ cup/170 g/5¹/₂ oz honey
1 cup/250 mL/8 fl oz orange juice
2 egg whites

1   Place oats, Weet-Bix (Weetabix), raisins and apricots in a bowl and mix to combine.

2   Place honey and orange juice in a small saucepan and bring to the boil over a medium heat. Reduce heat and simmer for 8-10 minutes or until mixture is thick and syrupy.

3   Stir honey mixture into oats mixture, then mix in egg whites.

4   Press mixture into a nonstick 18 x 28 cm/7 x 11 in tin lined with nonstick baking paper and bake for 20-25 minutes or until golden. Cool in tin, then cut into bars and store in an airtight container.

535 kilojoules (127 Calories) per serve
Carbohydrate	26.3 g (81%)	very high
Fat	1.3 g	very low

Cheese and Chive Scones

Makes 12-14
Oven temp: 180°C, 350°F, Gas 4

3 cups/375 g/12 oz self-raising flour
30 g/1 oz grated Parmesan cheese
45 g/1¹/₂ oz grated reduced-fat Cheddar cheese
3 tablespoons snipped fresh chives
freshly ground black pepper
¹/₄ cup/45 g/1¹/₂ oz low-fat natural yogurt
³/₄ cup/185 mL/6 fl oz skim milk

1   Place flour, Parmesan and Cheddar cheeses, chives and black pepper to taste in a bowl. Stir in yogurt and milk to form a soft sticky dough.

2   Turn dough onto a lightly floured surface and knead lightly. Press dough out to a 3 cm/1¹/₄ in thickness and, using a scone cutter, cut out 5 cm/2 in rounds. Place scones on a nonstick baking tray and bake for 12-15 minutes or until scones are risen and golden.

568 kilojoules (135 Calories) per serve
Carbohydrate	23 g (68%)	high
Fat	2 g	very low

READING LABELS

▶   Ingredients on labels are listed in order of quantity, so ingredients higher on the list are present in larger amounts than ingredients lower down.

▶   Food labels cannot include any nutrition claims such as 'salt-reduced' or 'low-fat' unless a nutrition information panel is on the packaging. Compare the nutrition panels of different products to hunt out the products which contain less fat, sugar or salt (sodium).

▶   What do the following claims mean?:

Lite – the characteristic which makes the food 'lite' must be stated on the label. Beware, it may be lighter in colour, taste or texture. If 'lite' refers to the energy (kilojoules/calories), fat or sugar level then the product must be either 'reduced' or 'low' in energy or the nutrient stated to be 'lite'.

Cholesterol Free – the food must not contain more than 3 mg of cholesterol per 100 g of food and must be either low in fat or have a fatty acid profile recommended for cholesterol lowering.

▶   Compare the amount of fat and salt between products using the information per 100 g of food. In general, look for products which provide:

less than 10 g fat/100 g (or the lowest fat product by comparison)

less than 120 mg salt/100 g

Cheese and Chive Scones, Banana Muffins, Muesli Bars

Spicy Chickpeas

Serves 4
Oven temp: 180°C, 350°F, Gas 4

2 teaspoons olive oil
¹/₂ teaspoon chilli powder
2 teaspoons ground cumin
2 teaspoons paprika
2 teaspoons ground coriander
freshly ground black pepper
4 cups/750 g/1¹/₂ lb cooked chickpeas

1   Heat oil in a small frying pan, add chilli powder, cumin, paprika, coriander and black pepper to taste and cook, stirring, for 2 minutes.

2   Add spice mixture to chickpeas and toss to combine. Spread chickpeas over the base of a shallow ovenproof dish and bake for 1 hour or until crunchy. Cool and store in an airtight container.

Cook's tip: Canned chickpeas can be used to make this recipe. Wash and drain chickpeas well before using.

850 kilojoules (205 Calories) per serve
Carbohydrate	24 g (47%)	low
Fat	6 g	low

Pitta Crisps

Serves 4
Oven temp: 180°C, 350°F, Gas 4

4 pitta bread rounds, split
90 g/3 oz grated Parmesan cheese
chilli powder or dried mixed herbs

Place bread rounds on baking trays. Sprinkle each round with Parmesan cheese, then with chilli powder or mixed herbs and bake for 10 minutes or until golden and crisp. Break into pieces, allow to cool and store in an airtight container.

Nutrition tip: These crisps are a great low-fat alternative to potato crisps or corn chips. Eat them on their own or bake plain crisps and serve with dips. For the best flavour use fresh Parmesan cheese.

985 kilojoules (235 Calories) per serve
Carbohydrate	33 g (56%)	high
Fat	6 g	low

Honey Soy Noodles

Serves 4

4 x 85 g/3 oz packets instant Chinese noodles
4 tablespoons honey
¹/₃ cup/90 mL/3 fl oz low-salt soy sauce
2 spring onions, finely chopped

1   Place noodles in a bowl, cover with boiling water and set aside to stand for 3-4 minutes or until soft.

2   Place honey, soy sauce and spring onions in a small saucepan and cook, stirring, over a medium heat for 2-3 minutes or until mixture thickens. Drain noodles, add sauce and toss to combine.

Cook's tip: Instant Chinese noodles are available from Oriental food stores or in the Oriental section of supermarkets. It is best to choose the Chinese noodles rather those that come with a flavour sachet as these contain fat.

1815 kilojoules (431 Calories) per serve
Carbohydrate	95 g (87%)	very high
Fat	1 g	very low

Pitta Crisps, Spicy Chickpeas

Bat Rebel Sports   Bowl Pillivuyt

Tuna and Corn Noodles

Serves 4

4 x 85 g/3 oz packets instant Chinese noodles
1/2 cup/125 mL/4 fl oz prepared tomato pasta sauce
2 x 125 g/4 oz canned sweet corn kernels, drained
220 g/7 oz canned tuna in springwater, drained and flaked

1   Place noodles in a bowl, cover with boiling water and set aside to stand for 3-4 minutes or until soft.

2   Place tomato sauce, sweet corn and tuna in a small saucepan and cook, stirring, over a medium heat for 2-3 minutes or until heated through. Drain noodles, add sauce and toss to combine.

1755 kilojoules (451 Calories) per serve

Carbohydrate	*73.5 g (70%)*	*very high*
Fat	*3 g*	*very low*

SNACK RIGHT

▶ Snack, don't pick! Nibbling little bits and pieces will feel less satisfying, plus you have no idea what you have eaten or how much.

▶ Snacks are fine, even when you are dieting. But remember to snack carefully on the right foods. Snack when you are hungry – not just because you're bored.

▶ Keep healthy snacks on hand. Make up some of the snack recipes in this section and keep them for a treat. You will then be able to grab something quickly that is delicious yet good for you.

▶ A pre-training snack is a good idea, especially for younger children, who tend to get hungry between meals. The right snack will boost energy levels and performance at training.

▶ If you can't resist crisps, biscuits or chocolates, don't bring them home from the supermarket.

Honey Soy Noodles,
Tuna and Corn Noodles

Bowls and Fork Country Road

Apple Toast Turnovers

Makes 12
Oven temp: 180°C, 350°F, Gas 4

12 slices white or wholemeal bread, crusts removed
440 g/14 oz canned unsweetened pie apple or stewed apple
1/4 cup/45 g/1 1/2 oz brown sugar
1/2 teaspoon ground cinnamon
60 g/2 oz sultanas
1 tablespoon honey
1 tablespoon hot water

1   Using a rolling pin, roll bread until flat.

2   Place apple, sugar, cinnamon and sultanas in a bowl and mix to combine.

3   Place a spoonful of apple mixture in the centre of each bread slice. Bring two opposite corners together and secure with a toothpick. Place bread parcels on a nonstick baking tray.

4   Combine honey and water and mix to dissolve honey. Brush each bread parcel with honey mixture and bake for 10-15 minutes or until golden and crisp.

525 kilojoules (125 Calories) per serve
Carbohydrate   26 g (83%)   very high
Fat   1 g   very low

Apricot Toast Turnovers

Replace pie apple with 440 g/14 oz canned unsweetened pie apricots.

480 kilojoules (115 Calories) per serve
Carbohydrate   23 g (83%)   very high
Fat   1 g   very low

TOPPING UP

Snack on carbohydrate foods to help you top up your energy levels. Try some of the following:

▶   Bread or toast, including raisin bread, crumpets, English muffins.

▶   Breakfast cereal with reduced-fat milk or low-fat yogurt, topped with fruit.

▶   Creamed rice – leftover rice mixed with reduced-fat milk or low-fat yogurt.

▶   Fresh, canned or dried fruit.

▶   Drink your snack. See page 31 for delicious drink ideas.

Pikelets

Makes 25

1 cup/125 g/4 oz self-raising flour
1 cup/155 g/5 oz wholemeal self-raising flour
1/4 cup/60 g/2 oz caster sugar
1 egg
1 1/2 cups/375 mL/12 fl oz skim milk
1 tablespoon finely grated lemon rind

1   Sift together self-raising and wholemeal self-raising flours into a bowl, return husks to bowl, add sugar and make a well in the centre of flour mixture. Combine egg, milk and lemon rind, pour into well and mix until batter is smooth.

2   Heat a nonstick frying pan over a medium heat and cook tablespoons of mixture for 1-2 minutes each side or until golden.

220 kilojoules (50 Calories) per pikelet
Carbohydrate   10 g (77%)   very high
Fat   0.5 g   very low

Blueberry Pikelets

Fold 90 g/3 oz fresh blueberries into batter before cooking.

230 kilojoules (55 Calories) per pikelet
Carbohydrate   11 g (78%)   very high
Fat   0.5 g   very low

Lemon and Currant Pikelets

Fold an extra 1/2 tablespoon finely grated lemon rind and 170 g/5 1/2 oz currants into batter before cooking.

300 kilojoules (75 Calories) per pikelet
Carbohydrate   15 g (82%)   very high
Fat   0.5 g   very low

Quick Banana Rice Custard

Serves 4

1 cup/220 g/7 oz short-grain rice
3 cups/750 mL/1 1/4 pt water
2 cups/500 mL/16 fl oz reduced-fat milk
2 tablespoons custard powder blended with 2 tablespoons water
2 tablespoons sugar
2 bananas, chopped
ground cinnamon

1   Place rice, water and milk in a saucepan and bring to the boil. Reduce heat and simmer, stirring occasionally, for 12-15 minutes or until rice is tender.

2   Stir in custard powder mixture and sugar and cook for 2-3 minutes longer. Add banana and mix to combine. Spoon rice into serving bowls and sprinkle with cinnamon.

Microwave it: Place rice, water and milk in a large microwave-safe container and cook on HIGH (100%) for 10-12 minutes or until rice is tender. Stir in custard powder mixture and sugar and cook for 1-2 minutes longer. Add banana and mix to combine.

1400 kilojoules (335 Calories) per serve
Carbohydrate   73 g (86%)   very high
Fat   0.5 g   very low

Right: Pikelets, Apple Toast Turnovers
Below: Quick Banana Rice Custard

Bowl and Fork Country Road   Goggles Rebel Sports

Green Plate Country Road   Blue Plate Limoges   Handweights Rebel Sports

CARBOHYDRATE
THE KEY TO ENERGY AND RECOVERY

Why Carbohydrate?

Benefits of high-carbohydrate eating:

▶ **Readily available**
Carbohydrate is the most readily available fuel for exercise.

▶ **Best fuel source**
While fat, and to a lesser extent protein, can be used for fuel, it is carbohydrate that is the number one fuel source for physical activity. It is carbohydrate that is solely burnt in the earlier stages of exercise and during periods where the intensity of exercise is high. No matter what your sport, carbohydrate is the best fuel source for maximum energy.

▶ **Fights fatigue**
The body stores carbohydrate as glycogen in the liver and muscles. The greater the intensity and duration of exercise, the greater the demand on the carbohydrate (glycogen) stores. If the body's carbohydrate stores are inadequate, fatigue sets in and performance falls.

▶ **Essential for health and fitness**
Carbohydrate foods like bread, breakfast cereal, rice, pasta, fruit and vegetables have a vital health role. These foods supply a wide range of nutrients, are lower in fat and are excellent sources of dietary fibre. In the interests of health and fitness eat at least 60% of your daily energy as carbohydrate.

Which carbohydrate is best?

We all have a daily kilojoule (calorie) budget. In many ways this is similar to our financial budget. When we shop we aim to get the best quality and value for our money. This should be the aim when we choose the foods we eat. The more vitamins and minerals we consume within our kilojoule (calorie) budget, the more nutrient rich is our diet. Just as we learn to recognise products which are value for money, we should also learn to recognise foods which provide maximum nutrients for each kilojoule (calorie).

Nutrient high carbohydrate foods include: bread, wholegrain breakfast cereal, rice, pasta, fruit and starchy vegetables like potato, corn and dried peas and beans. Foods which are high in carbohydrate but not nutrient rich include: soft drink, cordial, confectionery, fancy cakes and biscuits. When choosing carbohydrate foods remember to select nutrient rich carbohydrates for maximum health, vitality and energy.

The Glycaemic Index (GI) – the race between carbohydrates

Most people are familiar with the terms 'complex' and 'simple' carbohydrate. It was once believed that 'complex' carbohydrate (starch) found in bread, breakfast cereal, rice, pasta, potatoes and dried beans and peas sustained blood glucose levels more effectively than 'simple' carbohydrate (sugars). Research now proves this is a myth.

The absorption of carbohydrate from food and its effect on blood sugar (glycaemic response) is not predicted by its sugar or starch content as we have always been lead to believe. For example, the rise in blood sugar after eating bread is similar to after eating table sugar (sucrose). A number of factors such as the type of starch or sugar contained in the food, the processing and cooking of the food as well as the presence of fat and fibre influence the rate of rise in blood sugar (glycaemic response).

The glycaemic index of a food is a ranking of that food between 0 and 100. The ranking is like the outcome of a race between carbohydrate foods. Glucose is known to enter the blood stream fastest and therefore has the highest point score – a glycaemic index ranking of 100. The carbohydrate from dried beans and peas (eg lentils, soya beans etc) is known to enter the body very slowly and therefore has a low glycaemic index. The glycaemic index for soya beans is only 18. Other carbohydrate containing foods come somewhere in-between. The table on page 18 shows the glycaemic index (GI) of some common carbohydrate containing foods.

Glycaemic Index and Sports Performance

Foods with a high glycaemic index produce a sharp rise in blood sugar level followed by a more gradual fall. Low glycaemic index foods produce a slower but much more sustained rise and fall in blood sugar. Knowledge of the glycaemic index is now used to aid sports performance. The consumption of a low glycaemic index meal 2 hours prior to sports performance has been shown to prolong endurance (see page 66). High glycaemic index foods appear better for replenishing muscle glycogen stores after exercise (page 19).

Further research is required to determine the extent of the application of glycaemic index to sport, especially the everyday eating of the athlete. It is clear that athletes need to consider more than how much carbohydrate they eat, they also need to consider the type and timing of the carbohydrate in their diet to ensure optimal performance.

GLYCAEMIC INDEX OF FOODS (Glucose = 100)

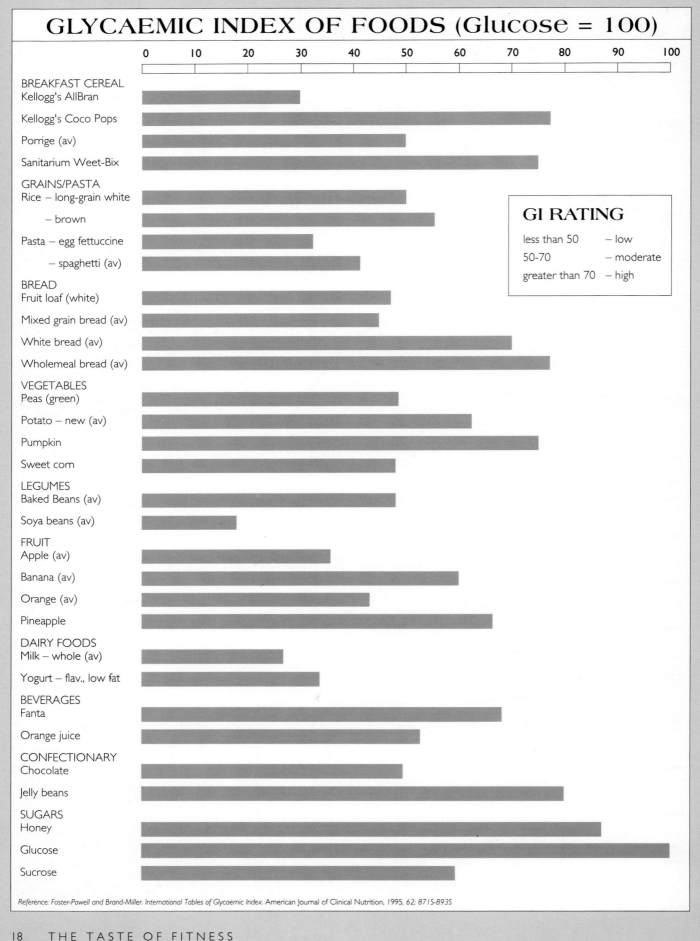

| | 0 | 10 | 20 | 30 | 40 | 50 | 60 | 70 | 80 | 90 | 100 |

GI RATING

less than 50	– low
50-70	– moderate
greater than 70	– high

BREAKFAST CEREAL
Kellogg's AllBran
Kellogg's Coco Pops
Porrige (av)
Sanitarium Weet-Bix

GRAINS/PASTA
Rice – long-grain white
        – brown
Pasta – egg fettuccine
         – spaghetti (av)

BREAD
Fruit loaf (white)
Mixed grain bread (av)
White bread (av)
Wholemeal bread (av)

VEGETABLES
Peas (green)
Potato – new (av)
Pumpkin
Sweet corn

LEGUMES
Baked Beans (av)
Soya beans (av)

FRUIT
Apple (av)
Banana (av)
Orange (av)
Pineapple

DAIRY FOODS
Milk – whole (av)
Yogurt – flav., low fat

BEVERAGES
Fanta
Orange juice

CONFECTIONARY
Chocolate
Jelly beans

SUGARS
Honey
Glucose
Sucrose

Reference: Foster-Powell and Brand-Miller. International Tables of Glycaemic Index. American Journal of Clinical Nutrition, 1995, 62; 871S-893S

Your Carbohydrate Needs

To estimate the amount of carbohydrate you require, multiply your weight by the suitable amount of carbohydrate shown in the table.

For example, if your activity level is moderate and you weigh 70 kg:

70 kg x 6-7 g carbohydrate/kg = 420-490 g of carbohydrate per day

Use the Carbohydrate Counter (page 90) to work out how much bread, fruit, pasta, rice, potato, cereal or other carbohydrate foods you will need to eat each day.

HOW MUCH CARBOHYDRATE?

The amount of carbohydrate you require depends on your weight and activity level. Use the following guide to work out how much you need each day.

Activity level*	Grams of carbohydrate/kg body weight/day
Light (less than 1 hour/day)	4-5
Light-moderate (1 hour/day)	5-6
Moderate (1-2 hours/day)	6-7
Moderate-heavy (2-4 hours/day)	7-8
Heavy (more than 4 hours/day)	8-10

* Note: Activity levels refer to the intensity as well as the duration of the activity. The time refers to the amount of time you are physically active during training, not the amount of time at training.

Carbohydrate and Recovery

After exercise, the muscles are hungry for carbohydrate. If carbohydrate intake is delayed, the muscles are starved of what they need most. Many sportspeople fail to feed their muscles soon enough after exercise. Instead, they take a shower, chat to their team mates and delay eating until they get home, usually more than an hour after training.

Eating or drinking carbohydrate soon (within 30 minutes) after strenuous aerobic-based exercise has been shown to enhance recovery by speeding up glycogen replacement. If you train hard each day, it is essential that you refuel your muscles promptly – there's no time to waste.

Most people find high-carbohydrate drinks easier to consume, as they are usually more thirsty than hungry after training or competition. A drink is generally more convenient than food and aids rehydration as well. Recovery will be incomplete if the body remains dehydrated (page 32).

EAT AND DRINK TO RECOVERY

Aim to consume approximately 1 g of carbohydrate/kg of body weight in the first two hours after exercise. In practical terms, this amounts to consuming around 50-100 g (more if your lean weight is over 100 kg) of carbohydrate every two hours until you are able to eat a high carbohydrate meal. Try for high glycaemic index carbohydrate at this time.

The following list of 50 g carbohydrate options will give you a few ideas of what to eat and drink. Remember you must also drink plenty of fluid to rehydrate.

Drinks

- 250 mL/8 fl oz high-carbohydrate sports drink such as a carbo loader drink
- 250-300 mL/8-9½ fl oz liquid meal such as Exceed Sports Meal or Sustagen Sport
- 500-1000 mL/16 fl oz-1¾ pt fluid-replacement drink (5-10% carbohydrate)
- 750 mL/1¼ pt cordial or 500 mL/16 fl oz soft drink, juice* or flavoured mineral water

Food

- 1-1½ jam or honey sandwiches
- 1 banana* sandwich
- 1 muffin (page 11)
- 1 Lebanese bread (24 cm/9½ in square)
- 2 medium-large bananas*
- 4 tablespoons sultanas*
- 2 Muesli Bars (page 11)
- 1 Sports bar

* Fructose sugar in fruit and juice does not seem to be as effective in replacing muscle glycogen stores as glucose.

LUNCHES
FOR PEAK PERFORMANCE

Citrus and Nectarine Salad

Serves 4

1 lettuce, leaves separated and torn into pieces
2 oranges, segmented
250 g/8 oz cherry tomatoes, halved
6 nectarines, stoned and quartered
1 red pepper, cut into strips
4 slices reduced-fat-and-salt ham, cut into strips

CITRUS DRESSING
1 tablespoon lemon juice
2 tablespoons orange juice
2 teaspoons sugar

1 Arrange lettuce, oranges, tomatoes, nectarines, red pepper and ham in a salad bowl.

2 To make dressing, place lemon juice, orange juice and sugar in a screwtop jar and shake to combine. Drizzle over salad and serve immediately.

Lunchbox tip: Place salad into a container and take dressing in a small jar. Just prior to serving, drizzle dressing over salad.

518 kilojoules (125 Calories) per serve
Carbohydrate   20 g (63%)   high
Fat   1 g   very low

Chicken Salad with Herb Mayonnaise

Serves 4

2 boneless chicken breast fillets
mixed lettuce leaves
60 g/2 oz snow pea sprouts or watercress
2 carrots, cut into strips
2 zucchini (courgettes) cut into strips
1 tomato, chopped

HERB DRESSING
4 tablespoons low-oil mayonnaise
3 tablespoons chopped fresh herbs of your choice

1 Heat a nonstick frying pan over a medium heat, add chicken and cook for 2-3 minutes each side or until cooked through. Remove chicken from pan and set aside to cool.

2 Cut chicken into strips. Arrange lettuce, snow pea sprouts or watercress, carrots, zucchini (courgettes) and tomato in a salad bowl.

3 To make dressing, combine mayonnaise and herbs and spoon over salad.

365 kilojoules (90 Calories) per serve
Carbohydrate   4 g (17%)   low
Fat   2 g   very low

Spinach and Pasta Salad

Serves 4

500 g/1 lb pasta of your choice
4 spring onions, finely chopped
8-10 stalks English spinach, chopped
2 tomatoes, chopped
155 g/5 oz reduced-fat feta cheese, chopped
12 button mushrooms sliced
1 red pepper, chopped

CHILLI DRESSING
2 tablespoons red wine vinegar
1 tablespoon sweet chilli sauce
1/4 cup/60 mL/2 fl oz no-oil French dressing

1 Cook pasta in boiling water in a large saucepan following packet directions. Drain, rinse under cold running water, then drain again and set aside to cool completely.

2 Place pasta, spring onions, spinach, tomatoes, feta cheese, mushrooms and red pepper in a salad bowl.

3 To make dressing, place vinegar, chilli sauce and French dressing in a screwtop jar and shake well to combine. Spoon dressing over salad and toss to combine.

2260 kilojoules (540 Calories) per serve
Carbohydrate   82 g (61%)   high
Fat   8 g   low

Chicken Salad with Herb Mayonnaise, Spinach and Pasta Salad, Citrus and Nectarine Salad

Salmon Bread Quiche

Serves 4
Oven temp: 180°C, 350°F, Gas 4

7 thick slices white or wholemeal bread, toasted and crusts removed

SALMON FILLING

4 eggs, lightly beaten
1½ cups/375 mL/12 fl oz reduced-fat milk
185 g/6 oz canned salmon in water, drained and flaked
1 tablespoon chopped fresh herbs of your choice
60 g/2 oz grated reduced-fat Cheddar cheese
freshly ground black pepper

1   Line a 23 cm/9 in square ovenproof dish with nonstick baking paper then with toast, cutting toast to fit.

2   To make filling, place eggs, milk, salmon, herbs, cheese and black pepper to taste in a bowl and mix to combine.

3   Pour filling into dish and bake for 25-30 minutes or until set and golden. Serve hot, warm or cold with salad.

1460 kilojoules (345 Calories) per serve
Carbohydrate	26 g (29%)	low
Fat	15 g	medium

Turkey Melts

Serves 2
Oven temp: 180°C, 350°F, Gas 4

4 slices wholegrain bread
2 tablespoons low-oil mayonnaise
1 small tomato, sliced
4 slices reduced-fat cooked turkey, cut into strips
2 tablespoons cranberry sauce
1 small red pepper, sliced
60 g/2 oz grated reduced-fat Swiss cheese

1   Spread bread with mayonnaise.

2   Top each slice of bread with tomato, turkey, cranberry sauce and red pepper then sprinkle with cheese.

3   Place on a nonstick baking tray and bake for 10-15 minutes or until crunchy and golden.

1160 kilojoules (275 Calories) per serve
Carbohydrate	28 g (39%)	low
Fat	8 g	low

Ham and Pineapple Melts

Serves 2
Oven temp: 180°C, 350°F, Gas 4

4 slices wholemeal bread
2 tablespoons low-oil mayonnaise
4 slices reduced-fat-and-salt ham, cut into thick strips
1 small green pepper, chopped
8 button mushrooms, sliced
220 g/7 oz canned unsweetened pineapple pieces, drained
60 g/2 oz grated reduced-fat Cheddar cheese

1   Spread bread with mayonnaise.

2   Top each slice of bread with ham, green pepper, mushrooms and pineapple, then sprinkle with cheese.

3   Place on a nonstick baking tray and bake for 10-15 minutes or until crunchy and golden.

1415 kilojoules (335 Calories) per serve
Carbohydrate	37 g (43%)	low
Fat	9.5 g	low

Delicious Sandwich Fillings

Avoid spreading bread with butter or margarine. Instead, try the following: low-oil mayonnaise, chutney, mustard, small amount of avocado, hummus.

▶   Snow pea sprouts or watercress, 10 g/¼ oz pâté and tomato

▶   Cottage cheese, ¼ avocado, tomato, lettuce and chilli sauce

▶   Fruit bread with banana, sultanas and cinnamon

▶   Lettuce, 45 g/1½ oz salmon, low-oil mayonnaise, gherkins and grated carrot

▶   Lettuce, 1 hard-boiled egg, low-oil mayonnaise mixed with curry powder

▶   Red pepper, 45 g/1½ oz drained canned tuna in springwater, pickles, lettuce and bean sprouts

▶   Hummus, tabbouleh and 1 slice reduced-fat Cheddar cheese

▶   Lean lamb, mint jelly and salad

▶   Lean rare roast beef, wholegrain mustard, lettuce, tomato and cucumber

BASICALLY BREAD

Bread is a nutritious food and health experts agree that we should all be eating more of it.

▶   Bread is not fattening; in fact, it is low in fat and sugar and contains significant quantities of protein, vitamins (especially thiamin), minerals, carbohydrate and dietary fibre.

▶   For interest, use a variety of breads.

▶   For a more filling sandwich, make a double-decker sandwich using three slices of bread instead of two. Why not try using different varieties of bread in one sandwich; for example, use one slice of white and two slices of wholegrain or wholemeal.

▶   The glycaemic index of bread varies according to the type of grain used. Breads containing barley, oats or those with heavy coarse grains have a lower glycaemic index than regular white or wholegrain bread.

▶   Bread keeps well in the freezer and if you like to eat a variety of breads this is a good way to store them. It is easy to remove just one or two slices as bread thaws quickly at room temperature or in the microwave.

▶   Freezing does not affect the nutritional value of bread.

Sandwiches with delicious and healthy fillings, Salmon Bread Quiche, Ham and Pineapple Melts, Turkey Melts,

Chicken Satay Roll-Ups

Serves 2

2 pitta bread rounds
2 lettuce leaves, shredded
1 small tomato, sliced
1 small green pepper, sliced
60 g/2 oz chopped cooked chicken

SATAY SAUCE
1 tablespoon peanut butter
1/4 teaspoon ground cumin
2 tablespoons low-oil mayonnaise
1 teaspoon low-salt soy sauce

1   To make sauce, place peanut butter, cumin, mayonnaise and soy sauce in a small bowl and mix to combine.

2   Top bread rounds with lettuce, tomato, green pepper and chicken. Spoon over sauce and roll up.

1165 kilojoules (395 Calories) per serve

Carbohydrate	53 g (53%)	medium
Fat	10 g	medium

Tuna Salad with Curry Mayonnaise

Serves 4

200 g/6¹/₂ oz broccoli, broken into florets
100 g/3¹/₂ oz snow peas (mangetout)
mixed lettuce leaves
2 cups/440 g/14 oz rice, cooked
440 g/14 oz canned tuna in water, drained and flaked
1 red pepper, chopped
1 yellow or green pepper, chopped
2 carrots, chopped

CURRY DRESSING
1/2 cup/125 mL/4 fl oz low-oil mayonnaise
2 teaspoons curry powder

1   Boil, steam or microwave broccoli and snow peas (mangetout) separately until just tender. Drain and refresh under cold running water.

2   Line a salad bowl with lettuce leaves. Combine rice, tuna, red pepper, yellow or green pepper, carrots, broccoli and snow peas (mangetout) and arrange on lettuce leaves.

3   To make dressing, place mayonnaise and curry powder in a bowl and mix to combine. Drizzle dressing over salad. Serve immediately or cover and chill.

1535 kilojoules (365 Calories) per serve

Carbohydrate	49 g (52%)	medium
Fat	4.5 g	very low

Spicy Salad Pockets

Serves 2

2 small pocket bread rounds

SALAD FILLING
6 curly endive or lettuce leaves
1 tomato, sliced
1 small cucumber, sliced
15 g/¹/₂ oz snow pea sprouts or watercress
1 small carrot, grated
45 g/1¹/₂ oz grated reduced-fat Cheddar cheese

Cloth Country Road   Plate Lifestyle Impacts

¹/₄ cup/60 mL/2 fl oz low-oil mayonnaise
2 teaspoons chilli sauce
2 teaspoons chopped fresh coriander

1   To make dressing, place mayonnaise, chilli sauce and coriander in a small bowl and mix to combine.

2   Make a small slit in the side of each bread round and fill with endive or lettuce, tomato, cucumber, snow pea sprouts or watercress, carrot and cheese. Drizzle with a little mayonnaise.

Cook's tip: The Spicy Dressing will keep in the refrigerator for several days and is delicious used as a dressing for your favourite salad or sandwiches.

980 kilojoules (235 Calories) per serve

Carbohydrate	31 g (43%)	low
Fat	6 g	low

Perfect Potato Salad

Serves 4

1 kg/2 lb baby new potatoes
2 leeks, finely sliced

FRESH HERB DRESSING
¹/₂ cup/125 mL/4 fl oz low-oil mayonnaise
¹/₄ cup/45 g/1¹/₂ oz low-fat natural yogurt
2 tablespoons snipped fresh chives
1 tablespoon chopped fresh dill
freshly ground black pepper

1   Bring a large saucepan of water to the boil, add potatoes and boil for 6-8 minutes or until tender. Drain potatoes and set aside to cool.

2   Place leeks in a nonstick frying pan and cook over a medium heat for 3-4 minutes or until golden. Cut potatoes in half and place in a bowl, add leeks and toss to combine.

3   To make dressing, place mayonnaise, yogurt, chives, dill and black pepper to taste in a bowl and mix to combine. Spoon dressing over salad and toss to combine. Chill well before serving.

670 kilojoules (160 Calories) per serve

Carbohydrate	31 g (79%)	very high
Fat	0.5 g	very low

Left: Chicken Satay Roll-Ups, Spicy Salad Pockets
Top right: Tuna Salad with Curry Mayonnaise
Right: Perfect Potato Salad

Plate Limoges   Towel Country Road   Goggles and Cap Rebel Sports

Bowl Orrefors Kosta Boda

BULKING UP
HOW TO BUILD BETTER BICEPS

Muscle-building pills and potions make a lot more money than muscle! The following Bulking-Up Brief gives you the scientific facts that could save you a lot of wasted time, effort and money.

BULKING-UP BRIEF

This will help you to build better biceps. Go for it!

Step 1

Training

▶ Obtain a professionally planned weight-training program.

▶ Aerobic training may need to be reduced (this will leave more fuel available for muscle growth).

▶ Make use of the 'off season' – it's easier to devote more attention to weight training then.

Step 2

Increase energy (kilojoule/calorie) intake

▶ Don't skip meals.

▶ Snack between meals (see page 11 for snack ideas). Remember if you are too full to eat, try a liquid meal instead (page 31).

▶ Drink high-energy drinks e.g. sports drinks – especially high-carbohydrate and milk-based sports drinks, reduced-fat milk and juices, instead of water, tea or coffee.

▶ If feeling too full is a problem, reduce your fibre intake. For example replace some wholegrain foods with more refined foods. Eat white bread, and cereals such as Cornflakes, Rice Bubbles (Crispies) and Special K instead of wholegrain bread and high-fibre cereals.

▶ Get organised. Prepare some meals and snacks ahead of time and keep them close by so there's less chance you'll skip them.

Step 3

Balancing protein, fat and carbohydrate

▶ Don't binge on protein, but do include a protein choice at each meal.

▶ Remember, protein intake will naturally increase to a sufficient level once you're eating more food.

▶ Carbohydrate provides energy – the body will use muscle protein for fuel if your carbohydrate intake is too low.

▶ Keep fat intake low to prevent gains in body fat.

Step 4

Monitoring progress

▶ Expect gains in the range of up to 0.5 kg/1 lb a week.

▶ Remember that rapid gains include undesirable body fat.

▶ If possible, monitor body fat with a skinfold (pinch) test (see page 78).

▶ Be patient – gaining muscle takes time.

Athletes refer to muscle gain as 'bulking up'. Athletes may want to bulk up:

▶ to increase strength for sports performance;

▶ to protect against injury – especially in body contact sports such as football;

▶ to improve physique – just to look and feel better.

It would seem to most people entering a weight-training gym that the secret to 'bulking up' lies in one of the umpteen supplements or containers of weight gain powder. Supplementation is advertised widely and promoted heavily by the anecdotes of 'Mr Universe' athletes. Their testimonials are supported financially, but not scientifically! The secret of success lies in the correct combination of diet and weight training. Weight training stimulates muscle growth, the diet provides the nutrients needed for growth and the fuel necessary for training.

As muscle is made of protein, athletes often think that a massive protein intake is necessary for massive muscle growth. The facts are that the body can only use a limited amount of protein each day. The excess is treated as waste and is excreted in the urine. This excess protein places an extra, unnecessary load on the kidneys. If the protein foods chosen contain fat or cholesterol (e.g. eggs, meat, full-cream milk) then the diet will also be high in fat. Research studies have found high levels of cholesterol in the blood of athletes following these high-protein diets. Use of anabolic steroids for muscle bulking, contributes to elevated cholesterol levels and further increases the risk for heart disease.

'Why do I have difficulty gaining muscle bulk?'

Physical activity burns up energy. If your food intake is insufficient then the body uses its stores of energy in the form of fat and muscle to keep it going. Young males in particular have high energy requirements; strenuous training increases their needs even further.

Often these requirements are more than the appetite allows, so it becomes difficult to consume the amount of food fuel needed to replace what is used up, let alone eat the extra amount necessary to fuel muscle growth. Frequently, strenuous training and busy work schedules take up valuable eating time. Some athletes also feel uncomfortable eating a snack prior to exercise and may not feel hungry until several hours after training.

If you are having difficulty bulking up use the Bulking-Up Brief on page 26 to help you get on the right track.

Body-Builder Drinks

Liquid supplements are useful in that they are quick, easy and tend not to fill you up too much. They are therefore an easy way to get extra energy (kilojoules/calories). The body-builder varieties tend to place too much emphasis on protein. Your own homemade drinks (see page 31) are better balanced and will be substantially cheaper. Commercially available liquid meals such as Exceed Sports Meal and Sustagen Sport are suitable if you don't want to make your own.

DID YOU KNOW?

Exercise increases protein needs. As a guide requirements are as follows:
◗ Sedentry Adult: 0.75 g protein/kg body weight/day
◗ Endurance or Strength Athlete: 1.5-1.7 g protein/kg body weight/day
◗ Bulking-up: 2 g protein/kg body weight/day

Vegetarians Take Note

There are particular nutrients which may be at risk in vegetarian diets. Iron and zinc intake tends to be lower than in meat eating diets. Calcium may be at risk when milk and dairy foods are avoided. Vegan vegetarian diets (containing no dairy foods or eggs) may not provide sufficient vitamin B_{12} so a supplement of this vitamin may be required. Providing foods like dried peas and beans, tofu, nuts and seeds are eaten together with ample quantities of breads and cereals, vegetarian diets will provide ample protein.

PROTEIN COUNTER

Food Description	Serve Size	Protein (g)
CEREALS		
Bread (average)	1 slice	2
Breakfast Cereal (average)	1 cup	4
Pasta, cooked (average)	1 cup	6
Rice, cooked (average)	1 cup	4
CHEESE		
Cheddar	30 g	7.5
Cheddar (reduced-fat)	30 g	8.5
Cottage (low-fat)	100 g	17.5
EGGS		
Raw egg (50 g)	1	6
FISH AND SEAFOOD		
Fish fillet	2 small fillets	36
Oysters	12	14.5
Prawns	1 cup, peeled	42.5
Salmon	220 g can	42.5
Tuna in brine	195 g can	43
FRUIT AND VEGETABLES		
Fruit (average)	1 piece	1
Vegetable (average)	1 average serve	2
MEATS		
Chicken breast fillet	100 g	22.5
Beef lean rump	180 g	57
Ham (leg)	1 slice	12.5
Hamburger patty	1 patty (average)	7
Lamb Chop (lean)	1 chump chop	18
Lamb Boneless (lean)	120 g	37
Pork butterfly steak	120 g	36
Turkey breast	120 g	36
MILK AND SOY PRODUCTS		
Skim	250 mL	9
2% fat	250 mL	10
Full fat	250 mL	8
Soy	250 mL	6
Soy lite	250 mL	7
NUTS AND LEGUMES		
Almonds	50 g	10
Baked beans	1 cup	14
Kidney beans	1 cup	21
Lentils	1 cup	16
Peanuts	50 g	12.5
Soya beans	1 cup	13
SPORT SUPPLEMENTS*		
Exceed Sports meal	100 g powder	16
Sustagen Sport	100 g powder	25

Source: Commonwealth Department of Community Services and Health 1991/1992, NUTTAB version 1991/1992. Food Industry Data.
* Data provided by manufacturer.

Amino Acid Supplements

The claims for amino acid supplements are growing, mainly as the result of clever marketing. 'Aminos' have been around for some time; however, there is really no substantial scientific support for their use. Amino acids are the building blocks of protein. Protein-rich foods are a much better source of amino acids than amino acid supplements. Claims that specific amino acid preparations stimulate growth hormone, have not been supported by scientific research.

Amino acid companies do not provide a money-back guarantee if amino acids don't work. Companies which sell pharmaceuticals are obligated to demonstrate the efficacy and safety of any product prior to it being approved for sale. As consumers, we would not expect any less. Yet when it comes to amino acids and countless other nutrition supplements, many people are willing to accept the advertising blurb as scientific proof.

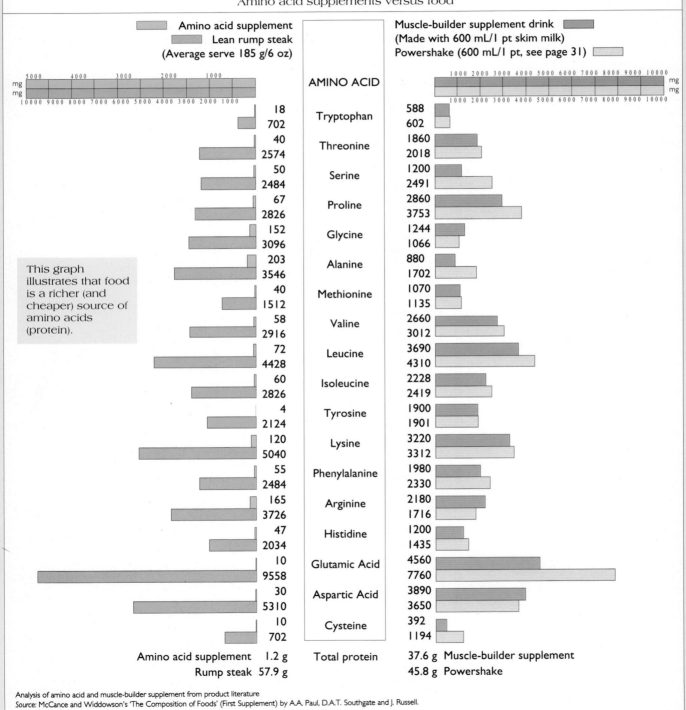

AMINO ACID COMPARISONS
Amino acid supplements versus food

Amino acid supplement
Lean rump steak
(Average serve 185 g/6 oz)

Muscle-builder supplement drink
(Made with 600 mL/1 pt skim milk)
Powershake (600 mL/1 pt, see page 31)

This graph illustrates that food is a richer (and cheaper) source of amino acids (protein).

AMINO ACID	Amino acid supplement	Lean rump steak	Muscle-builder supplement	Powershake
Tryptophan	18	702	588	602
Threonine	40	2574	1860	2018
Serine	50	2484	1200	2491
Proline	67	2826	2860	3753
Glycine	152	3096	1244	1066
Alanine	203	3546	880	1702
Methionine	40	1512	1070	1135
Valine	58	2916	2660	3012
Leucine	72	4428	3690	4310
Isoleucine	60	2826	2228	2419
Tyrosine	4	2124	1900	1901
Lysine	120	5040	3220	3312
Phenylalanine	55	2484	1980	2330
Arginine	165	3726	2180	1716
Histidine	47	2034	1200	1435
Glutamic Acid	10	9558	4560	7760
Aspartic Acid	30	5310	3890	3650
Cysteine	10	702	392	1194

Total protein:
Amino acid supplement 1.2 g
Rump steak 57.9 g
Muscle-builder supplement 37.6 g
Powershake 45.8 g

Analysis of amino acid and muscle-builder supplement from product literature
Source: McCance and Widdowson's 'The Composition of Foods' (First Supplement) by A.A. Paul, D.A.T. Southgate and J. Russell.

TEN DIETARY MISTAKES MADE BY ATHLETES

1 Skipping meals

Training can be very time consuming. Often meals are skipped when time just runs out. Unfortunately, this can mean that energy reserves also run out – just like a car running out of petrol. Use this book to help you organise food which is fast and healthy so you can quickly and easily refuel your body at each meal.

2 Not enough carbohydrate

Foods rich in carbohydrate – particularly nutritious carbohydrate – need to become the major food group that you eat at each meal. One big bowl of pasta in the evening is not enough. Include a variety of carbohydrate foods such as bread, cereal, rice, pasta, potatoes, fruit and juice at each meal. The tables on pages 19 and 90 will help you work out your carbohydrate needs.

3 Too much fat

One of the reasons why we may not eat enough carbohydrate is that we fill up on fat. The fat we eat is all too easily converted to body fat and cholesterol – leading to a higher prevalence of obesity and heart disease when fat intake is too high.

Some people who are lean and fit become blasé about eating fat. While they may be lean and have no cholesterol problems, diseases like gall stones and certain cancers (especially those of the breast and bowel) are also linked with eating too much fat.

If their high-fat diet continues and exercise doesn't, they'll end up wearing more fat than they burn off!

4 Too much salt

Even if you train hard and sweat a lot, your diet will provide adequate salt – there's no need to add any extra salt to your food. As you get fitter, you'will sweat more during exercise, this is because your body becomes better equipped to keep itself cool. The body manages to conserve salt by reducing the concentration of the salt in sweat (and urine). So the more you sweat, the less salty it gets.

5 Supplement addiction – are you hooked?

Athletic people often feel that they can't get by without supplements. They may do nothing about their food intake, thinking that supplements can make up for what they might be missing out on. The truth is that vitamin and mineral supplements do not make up for too little carbohydrate or too much fat. The only way to be well nourished is to eat well. Supplements have not been shown to improve athletic performance in well-nourished people. Large doses of vitamins and minerals can be toxic and may interfere with normal nutrient absorption. Nutrition supplements do have a role to play in some situations, see Vitamins and Minerals (page 81).

6 Don't rely on your thirst

Fluid intake should be adequate to replace what is lost as sweat. Your thirst is not a good indicator of how much fluid you need – by the time you feel thirsty, you are already dehydrated. Dehydration decreases athletic performance – it's also dangerous. See page 32 for more information.

7 Fibre – too much of a good thing?

Fibre is nature's natural appetite suppressant, it helps you to feel full and to moderate your intake. It also exercises your bowel and helps to keep you regular. Too much fibre, however, is not a good thing. For a start, you will feel bloated and won't be able to get through the day without numerous trips to the bathroom.

Active people who exercise regularly and include liberal amounts of wholegrains, vegetables and fruit in their diet do not need unprocessed bran or fibre supplements. In fact, they may need to substitute wholegrains with some 'white' varieties of bread, cereal, rice or pasta. They may be getting more fibre than their bowel can handle. Fibre is a good thing, but don't go overboard.

8 Dieting – on the edge

Most of us are not perfectly happy with our shape. Generally, it's the body fat which frustrates us the most, perhaps to the point of desperation. It's at this stage that we are more susceptible to fad diets and their promises of quick and easy weight loss.

Sometimes even sensible dieting can get out of hand. For example, low-fat turns into no-fat, and little by little the amount of food eaten dwindles to almost nothing. Energy levels slide, yet weight may not budge. Dieting 'on the edge' is dangerous, ineffective in the long term and will leave its mark both physically and psychologically. For safe, sensible and successful approaches see page 78.

9 Being too pure

We've all met at least one; the person who controls every urge to sneak a morsel of fat, sugar or salt. They never put a tooth near a chocolate bar, cake or ice cream. While their dedication to perfect eating is admirable, it's not optimal and it's certainly anti-social.

Being sensible about your diet means you can splurge now and then. This helps to keep you in balance socially and mentally. We all need to relax a little sometimes so we can enjoy the full benefits of training and life.

10 Comparing intakes

The amount of food needed varies widely between people. Even if age, sex, height, weight and physical activity are taken into account, there are still individual factors. Some lucky people therefore just need to eat more than others. If you constantly compare yourself to others you may get frustrated and lose focus of what is right for you.

Glasses Home and Garden on the Mall and Country Road

DRINKS
ENERGY IN A GLASS

Chocolate Milkshake

Serves 1

1 cup/250 mL/8 fl oz reduced-fat milk
2 tablespoons low-fat vanilla yogurt
1 tablespoon skim milk powder
2 tablespoons chocolate topping (sauce) or
2 tablespoons chocolate drink powder

Place milk, yogurt, milk powder and chocolate topping or chocolate drink powder in a food processor or blender and process until thick and frothy. Pour into a serving glass and serve immediately.

1260 kilojoules (400 Calories) per serve
Carbohydrate   50 g (63%)   high
Fat   4.5 g   very low

Caramel Milkshake
Replace chocolate topping (sauce) with 2 tablespoons caramel topping (sauce).

1195 kilojoules (285 Calories) per serve
Carbohydrate   45 g (62%)   high
Fat   5 g   low

Vanilla Milkshake
Replace chocolate topping (sauce) with 1 teaspoon vanilla essence.

850 kilojoules (200 Calories) per serve
Carbohydrate   25 g (47%)   low
Fat   4.5 g   very low

Strawberry Milkshake
Replace chocolate topping (sauce) with 8 fresh strawberries or 2 tablespoons strawberry topping (sauce).

1195 kilojoules (285 Calories) per serve
Carbohydrate   46 g (62%)   high
Fat   4.5 g   very low

Mango Smoothie

Serves 1

1 cup/250 mL/8 fl oz reduced-fat milk
1/4 cup low-fat vanilla yogurt
1 tablespoon skim milk powder
2 teaspoons honey (optional)
4 ice cubes
1/2 mango, stoned, peeled and chopped

Place milk, yogurt, milk powder, honey (if using), ice cubes and mango in a food processor or blender and process until smooth. Pour into a serving glass and serve immediately.

1240 kilojoules (295 Calories) per serve
Carbohydrate   47 g (61%)   high
Fat   5 g   low

Banana Smoothie
Replace mango with 1 banana.

1570 kilojoules (375 Calories) per serve
Carbohydrate   65 g (67%)   high
Fat   5 g   low

Peach and Apricot Smoothie
Replace mango with 1 peeled and sliced peach and 2 chopped apricots.

1425 kilojoules (340 Calories) per serve
Carbohydrate   55 g (63%)   high
Fat   5 g   low

Watermelon Crush

Serves 1

10 ice cubes
1 tablespoon lemon juice
500 g/1 lb chopped watermelon

Place ice cubes, lemon juice and watermelon in a food processor or blender and process until smooth. Pour into a serving glass and serve immediately.

485 kilojoules (115 Calories) per serve
Carbohydrate   25 g (86%)   very high
Fat   1 g   very low

Melon Crush
Replace watermelon with 500 g/1 lb chopped rockmelon (cantaloupe) and honeydew melon.

464 kilojoules (110 Calories) per serve
Carbohydrate   24 g (86%)   very high
Fat   0.5 g   very low

Pineapple Crush
Replace watermelon with 500 g/1 lb chopped pineapple and 1 tablespoon chopped fresh mint.

1535 kilojoules (365 Calories) per serve
Carbohydrate   84 g (93%)   very high
Fat   0 g   nil

Mixed Fruit Crush
Replace watermelon with 1 chopped orange, 1 chopped banana and 1 chopped kiwifruit.

855 kilojoules (205 Calories) per serve
Carbohydrate   45.5 g (88%)   very high
Fat   0.5 g   very low

Powershake

Serves 1

1 cup/250 mL/8 fl oz reduced-fat milk
3 tablespoons low-fat vanilla yogurt
2 tablespoons skim milk powder
2 tablespoons unprocessed bran
1 tablespoon wheat germ
2 teaspoons honey
1 banana, chopped
4 ice cubes

Place milk, yogurt, milk powder, bran, wheat germ, honey, banana and ice cubes in a food processor or blender and process until smooth. Pour into a serving glass and serve immediately.

1900 kilojoules (450 Calories) per serve
Carbohydrate   74 g (63%)   high
Fat   6 g   low

FIBRE

Reasons for choosing a high-fibre diet.

▶ Fibre, especially the fibre found in breads and cereals, promotes normal bowel action and prevents constipation.

▶ Blood cholesterol levels may be reduced by the soluble fibre found in fruits and vegetables, particularly the legumes, as well as rice, barley and oats.

▶ Fibre promotes fullness. High-fibre foods help to satisfy the appetite and prevent overeating.

▶ There is evidence to suggest that a high-fibre intake reduces the risk of bowel cancer.

Watermelon Crush, Strawberry Milkshake, Pineapple Crush, Mango Smoothie, Mixed Fruit Crush, Chocolate Milkshake

KEEP COOL
WHEN THE HEAT'S ON

Sweating helps you keep cool during exercise, just like the radiator of a car keeps the engine cool. When there's not enough water in the radiator, the car overheats – just as you do when you're dehydrated.

Overheating or heat stress during exercise decreases performance. Severe heat stress is dangerous. Permanent physical damage, even death, can eventuate if fluid intake is neglected. Even the fittest athletes can get caught out.

'How much fluid do I need to drink?'

Fluid requirements for exercise differ according to the amount of sweat lost. The most accurate way of working out your fluid requirements is by measuring your pre- and post-exercise weight. Your body is about 60% water and each 1 litre/1¾ pt of water weighs about 1 kg/2 lb. The amount of weight you lose during exercise corresponds to the amount of water lost as sweat. Any amount of fluid loss during exercise is detremental to performance no matter how small; losses of 5% or more are extremely dangerous. Aim to replace your fluid losses as you go. As it is difficult to replace all of the sweat lost during exercise a general safety limit is to keep fluid losses less than 2% of body weight e.g. a 70 kg/11 stone person should aim to keep fluid loss during an event to less than 2% of 70 kg/11 stone, which is about 1.4 kg/3 lb.

Top up – don't guzzle

Don't wait until you are thirsty to start drinking. During exercise, your thirst is a poor indicator of fluid needs. Drink regularly in small amounts. If you postpone drinking, you will have to drink too much too quickly to catch up. By this stage, dehydration may have already set in. Fluid empties more slowly from the stomach when you are dehydrated, so it may even be impossible to catch up while you are still exercising. Drinking small amounts of fluid regularly is far more comfortable than sculling large amounts all at once. The top-up method improves the rate at which fluid leaves the stomach, therefore the rate at which it can be absorbed. The best approach is to start exercise with a comfortably full level of fluid in your stomach and top up this level regularly.

Towels Country Road Sunscreens Clarins

Don't Let Dehydration Cramp Your Style

The cause of cramps is still unknown, however dehydration increases your chance of getting a cramp. Adequate fluid replacement will help to prevent most cramps.

'What about water?'

Water is a great fluid replacer, it is also easy and cheap to obtain. If you exercise for 2 hours or less at a time, drinking plain water to replace fluids is fine. For more prolonged training sessions or competitions, fluid-replacement drinks have the advantage of assisting with refuelling as well as hydration.

Fluid-Replacement Drinks

Experts in the 1970s said water was best, but now the benefits of fluid-replacement drinks for sport are being recognised. These benefits include:

Hydration: The glucose in fluid-replacement drinks, enhances water absorption from the intestine. This aids hydration.

Taste: People tend to prefer the flavour of sports drinks over plain water. The pleasant taste encourages them to drink more and replace fluid losses better.

Refuelling: The carbohydrate in fluid-replacement drinks helps to delay fatigue in endurance events. Athletes should aim to drink about 50 g of carbohydrate per hour. They can achieve this by drinking 500-1000 mL/16 fl oz-1¾ pt of a fluid-replacement drink which contains between 5-10% carbohydrate. Refuelling is easier and more rapid from liquids than solids (see page 19 for a list of suitable solid options).

Salt: The sodium in fluid-replacement drinks helps to maintain blood sodium levels in ultra-endurance athletes, where exercise duration and heavy sweating may span over many hours or days. Sodium replacement via a fluid-replacement drink is strongly recommended if the event involves 4 hours or more of strenuous activity.

A fluid-replacement drink only really needs to be a dilute solution of carbohydrate and salt, it does not need to contain fat or protein. Fluid-replacement drinks should ideally contain between 5-10% carbohydrate (5-10 g of carbohydrate per 100 mL/ 3½ fl oz drink). The carbohydrate in sports drinks may be in the form of sugars or glucose polymers (chains of glucose units). The main difference between these carbohydrate sources is taste, glucose polymers taste less sweet.

As too much salt tastes unpleasant, the salt (electrolyte) content of these drinks is generally okay. There are many sports drinks on the market, but not all of these are designed for fluid replacement. When choosing a fluid-replacement drink, read the label carefully and use the above guidelines to help you make the best choice. Drink your fluid-replacement drink cool, not icy cold.

Drinks like soft drink or fruit juice have a higher carbohydrate concentration (12-13%) and therefore empty more slowly from the stomach – they are not the best fluid replacers. These drinks can be used if they are diluted to half strength. Soft drinks should be defizzed (left to go flat) and not contain caffeine.

Rule of thumb

Most well-trained athletes lose around 1 litre/1¾ pt of sweat for each hour of intense physical exercise. You should aim to replace at least two-thirds of this amount whilst exercising. This means drinking about 600-750 mL/1-1¼ pt of fluid for each hour of strenuous exercise. Remember, if it's hot and/ or you sweat heavily, you may need to drink more than this.

Did you know?

In 1971 the first 'City to Surf' race was organised from Central Sydney to Bondi Beach. Twenty-nine of the 1,600 participants failed to complete the course due to the effects of heat exhaustion. Seven competitors required admission to hospital for a few days (Richards et al,. 1994).

GETTING TOO HOT IS NOT COOL

The symptoms of heat stress sneak up on you. Ignoring these symptoms is extremely dangerous, because if you have symptoms you are already quite dehydrated. Don't push yourself to boiling point. These symptoms are your body's way of telling you to stop.

Early warning signs include:
- feeling hot and tired
- muscle cramps
- nausea
- difficulties with concentration
- headache

As the condition worsens you may:
- feel dizzy
- become incoherent or disoriented
- stop sweating (skin becomes hot and dry)

Making it to the finish line does not prove that you were properly hydrated. Cramps, headaches or nausea after exercise are most likely caused by dehydration. Take heed of these warning signs and make sure that you replace your fluids adequately both during and after the event.

Severe heat stress requires urgent medical attention.

BE STRONG
SAY 'NO' TO ALCOHOL

Alcohol decreases performance. Some athletic people regularly binge on alcohol and still believe that excessive alcohol does not really affect them. Reasons given for excessive drinking include:

'It relaxes me and reduces nervousness'

Alcohol makes you less aware of what is happening, so you may feel more relaxed and less nervous; however, it has this effect on your whole nervous system, so:

your reflexes are slowed
your concentration is dulled
your judgement is impaired

The 'false confidence' you have after drinking alcohol may trick you into thinking you're doing your best when in fact your performance is impaired.

'I train it off or sweat it out'

While you may burn up the kilojoules (calories) alcohol contains, you can't sweat the alcohol out. Excess alcohol can affect many body systems, including:

the brain and nervous system
the heart
the liver

Training cannot reverse these effects. The aim of sports participation is to reach your personal peak, not stay where you are now. To train smart – you must train sober.

'I only drink after the game'

Binge drinking after competition is still common, especially in team sports. Most drinkers think this does no harm as they may 'hardly ever drink at other times'. Binge drinking is as much of a health risk as drinking too much on a regular basis. Exercise beforehand does not reduce your risk. From a fitness and performance point of view, alcohol after strenuous exercise delays recovery. This is because alcohol has a diuretic (dehydrating) effect and also delays the rate of glycogen replenishment. For many, the hangover after an alcohol binge affects their performance at training for several days. The loss of valuable training time is more than they or their team can afford.

Alcohol and injury don't mix

Alcohol dilates blood vessels so it can intensify the swelling and bleeding associated with many sports injuries. A stiff drink may temporarily help you psychologically, but alcohol potentially increases the extent of damage and will delay recovery time. Alcohol should be avoided in all cases of injury for at least 24 hours or until otherwise advised by your doctor.

ALCOHOL

Facts about alcohol you should know include:

▶ You can't sweat it out.
▶ It dehydrates you.
▶ It delays recovery.
▶ It impairs heat regulation.
▶ It slows down glycogen replacement.
▶ It delays recovery from soft tissue (bruising type) injuries.
▶ It depletes the body of important vitamins and minerals.
▶ It slows reaction time and reduces coordination.
▶ It is fattening.
▶ Alcohol is an addictive drug.

Drink Smart

If you drink sensibly, there is no reason why you can't enjoy alcohol regularly. Try these smart drinking tips:

During the week

▶ Enjoy a drink during the week if you compete each weekend.
▶ Drink no more than two standard drinks on any day (see chart).
▶ Try not to drink two days in a row.
▶ If you are watching your weight/ body fat levels, try to keep alcohol just for special occasions.

Precompetition

▶ Avoid alcohol 24 hours prior to competition.

After competition

▶ Rehydrate fully (see page 32) before drinking alcohol.
▶ Avoid drinking alcohol in the dressing room.
▶ Start glycogen replacement by consuming carbohydrate-rich foods or drinks as soon as possible after exercise (see page 19 for ideas).
▶ Avoid alcohol if you have been injured.
▶ Drink alcohol with a meal, not on an empty stomach.
▶ Drink a safe level of alcohol. If you have gone over the legal drink-driving limit, you've had too much.

Social ways to drink less

▶ Avoid getting into a 'Round' – why pay for everyone else to get drunk?
▶ Dilute drinks with water, soda or soft drink.
▶ Choose low-alcohol beers.
▶ Offer to drive – it gives you a good reason to drink less.
▶ Set yourself a limit before you start drinking.
▶ Be strong enough to say 'no'.

STANDARD DRINK
Approximately 10 g alcohol

DRINK	10 g ALCOHOL
Regular beer 5% alcohol	200 mL
Light beer 2-3% alcohol	2 × 200 mL
Extra light beer 1% alcohol	5 × 200 mL
Wine/Champagne 10-12% alcohol	100 mL
Spirits 30-40% alcohol	30 mL
Port/Sherry 15-20% alcohol	60 mL
Cider/Stout 5% alcohol	200 mL

Did you know?

When you have alcohol in your system you burn fat more slowly.

CALCIUM
AND OSTEOPOROSIS

Osteoporosis is a condition in which the bones lose calcium, become brittle and tend to break more easily. Our bones reach peak bone strength from late adolescence to early 20s.

▶ Bone loss accelerates in women for 5-10 years after menopause. An increased rate of bone loss may also occur in young athletic women if their menstrual cycle is infrequent or if it stops altogether (a condition known as amenorrhoea). The fall in oestrogen levels associated with cycle cessation is responsible for the increased rate of loss.

▶ Regular strenuous exercise, usually accompanied by other factors such as fat loss, strict dieting or stress, can precipitate cycle interruptions in young female athletes. In these women, the well-known benefits of exercise (particularly weight-bearing exercise such as walking, running and aerobic dance) on bone mass do not outweigh the losses which occur as a result of menstrual irregularity. The benefits of adequate or extra calcium are limited unless the menstrual cycle returns or a program of hormone replacement (usually the oral contraceptive pill in younger women) is undertaken.

▶ Lost bone is not so easy to replace. Menstrual irregularities of greater than six months need medical investigation, ideally by a doctor experienced in dealing with young female athletes. An adequate calcium intake throughout life together with a regular menstrual cycle and weight-bearing exercise is essential to build and then maintain optimal bone strength. Extra calcium in the range of 1000-1500 mg per day is recommended during, and for sometime after, the period of amenorrhoea. Calcium supplements may be needed to help some women reach this daily target.

Other factors detrimental to bone health include:

▶ Cigarette smoking

An excess intake of:

▶ salt;

▶ protein;

▶ caffeine e.g. coffee, tea, cola drinks, chocolate; and

▶ alcohol – two or more standard drinks a day. (See page 34 for standard drinks.)

Three serves of dairy food each day as part of a balanced diet will supply most people with the calcium they need. Calcium can be found in a large number of foods but often only in small amounts. Dairy foods are a richer source of calcium which is generally better absorbed by the body than the calcium from many other foods. There is a wide range of reduced-fat dairy foods to choose from. Low-fat milk and yogurt contain as much calcium as full-fat varieties and fortified milks have even more.

CALCIUM

Daily requirements mg/day

Age (years)	Males	Females
8-11	800	900
12-15	1200	900
16-18	1000	1000
19-54	800	800
54-64	800	1000
Pregnant	–	1100
Lactating	–	1200

DAIRY FOOD EQUIVALENTS
To provide 800 mg of calcium

milk 200 mL/6½ fl oz
full-fat 240 mg

yogurt 200 g/6½ oz
full-fat 390 mg

cheese 30 g/1 oz
Cheddar 234 mg

 +  +

1-2% fat 285 mg
skim 260 mg
fortified 320 mg

non-fat 340 mg

cottage* 300 g = 237 mg
ricotta* 100 g = 245 mg
*reduced-fat varieties

Use the table above to work out your calcium requirements. If necessary, add in extra servings of dairy food to reach your daily target.
Note: 200 mL/6½ fl oz fortified soy milk has 290 mg calcium. This is the best substitute if you are unable to eat dairy food.

DINNER
DELICIOUS WAYS TO RECHARGE

Tandoori Chicken

Serves 6
Oven temp: 180°C, 350°F, Gas 4

6 boneless chicken breast fillets, skin removed

TANDOORI PASTE
2 teaspoons ground cumin
I teaspoon ground coriander
¹/₂ teaspoon ground cardamom
I teaspoon grated fresh ginger
¹/₂ teaspoon ground turmeric
¹/₂ teaspoon chilli powder
I cup/200 g/6¹/₂ oz low-fat natural yogurt

1   To make Tandoori Paste, place cumin, coriander, cardamom, ginger, turmeric and chilli powder in a bowl and mix to combine. Add yogurt and mix to make a paste.

2   Place chicken in a shallow glass or ceramic dish, spoon over Tandoori Paste and turn to coat. Cover and set aside to marinate for 2 hours.

3   Remove chicken from Tandoori Paste, place in a baking dish and bake for 20-30 minutes or until chicken is cooked.

Serving suggestion: For a complete meal, serve Tandoori Chicken with rice and salad.

585 kilojoules (140 Calories) per serve
Carbohydrate	2 g (6%)	low
Fat	4 g	very low

Tandoori Lamb
Replace chicken fillets with 6 lamb fillets or lamb leg steaks.

975 kilojoules (235 Calories) per serve
Carbohydrate	2 g (3%)	low
Fat	7 g	low

Nachos

Serves 4
Oven temp: 180°C, 350°F, Gas 4

I quantity Spicy Beans (see page 44)
2 teaspoons chilli sauce
I quantity plain Pitta Crisps (see page 12)
60 g/2 oz grated reduced-fat mozzarella cheese
4 tablespoons low-fat natural yogurt

1   Make up Spicy Beans following recipe, adding chilli sauce.

2   Make up Pitta Crisps following recipe.

3   Place Pitta Crisps in an ovenproof baking dish, spoon over Spicy Beans and sprinkle with cheese. Bake for 10-15 minutes or microwave on HIGH (100%) for 2-3 minutes or until cheese melts. Serve with yogurt.

2355 kilojoules (560 Calories) per serve
Carbohydrate	77 g (54%)	medium
Fat	13 g	medium

Beef Skewers

Serves 4

750 g/1¹/₂ lb rump steak, cut into thin strips
2 cups/440 g/14 oz rice, cooked

HONEY MARINADE
I clove garlic, crushed
2 tablespoons honey
2 teaspoons curry powder
I tablespoon low-salt soy sauce

1   To make marinade, place garlic, honey, curry powder and soy sauce in a bowl and mix to combine. Add beef and toss to coat. Cover and set aside to marinate for 1 hour.

2   Preheat grill or barbecue to a medium-high heat. Thread beef strips on skewers and cook under grill or on barbecue, turning occasionally, for 4-5 minutes or until cooked to your liking. Serve with rice.

2605 kilojoules (620 Calories) per serve
Carbohydrate	91 g (58%)	high
Fat	5 g	low

Nachos, Beef Skewers, Tandoori Chicken

White Plate Pillivuyt Blue and Orange Plates Limoges

Pasta with Tomato, Chilli and Herb Sauce

Serves 4

500 g/1 lb pasta of your choice
TOMATO, CHILLI AND
HERB SAUCE
1 onion, chopped
2 cloves garlic, crushed
2 x 440 g/14 oz canned tomatoes,
undrained and mashed
3 tablespoons tomato paste (purée)
2 teaspoons chilli sauce
1 red pepper, chopped
1 green pepper, chopped
1 tablespoon chopped fresh basil
1 tablespoon chopped fresh parsley
freshly ground black pepper

1   Cook pasta in boiling water in a
large saucepan following packet
instructions. Drain, set aside and
keep warm.

2   To make sauce, place onion and
garlic in a nonstick frying pan and
cook, stirring, over a medium heat
for 2-3 minutes or until soft.

3   Stir in tomatoes, tomato paste
(purée), chilli sauce, red pepper,
green pepper, basil, parsley and
black pepper to taste and simmer
for 10 minutes or until sauce
reduces and thickens slightly.
Spoon sauce over pasta and serve
immediately.

1760 kilojoules (420 Calories) per serve
Carbohydrate   84.5 g (81%)   *very high*
Fat   1.5 g   *very low*

Pasta with Marinara Sauce

Serves 4

500 g/1 lb pasta of your choice
MARINARA SAUCE
8 large uncooked prawns, shelled and
deveined, tails left intact
8 mussels
1 tablespoon lemon juice
1 calamari (squid) tube, sliced
4 baby octopus, cleaned and chopped
1 quantity Tomato Chilli and Herb Sauce
(see recipe above) or 750 mL/1¹/₄ pt jar
prepared tomato pasta sauce

1   Cook pasta in boiling water in a
large saucepan following packet
instructions. Drain, set aside and
keep warm.

2   To make sauce, place prawns,
mussels and lemon juice in a
nonstick frying pan and cook,

stirring, over a medium-high heat for
3-4 minutes or until prawns just
change colour and are almost
cooked. Add calamari (squid) and
octopus and cook, stirring, for
1 minute longer.

3   Stir in sauce, bring to simmering
and cook for 2-3 minutes or until
heated through. Spoon sauce over
pasta and serve immediately.

2480 kilojoules (590 Calories) per serve
Carbohydrate   86 g (58%)   *high*
Fat   7 g   *low*

Pasta with Cheese Sauce

Serves 4

500 g/1 lb pasta of your choice
45 g/1¹/₂ oz grated Parmesan cheese
45 g/1¹/₂ oz grated reduced-fat Cheddar
cheese
BASIC WHITE SAUCE
1¹/₂ cups/375 mL/12 fl oz reduced-fat milk
¹/₂ cup/125 mL/4 fl oz chicken stock
¹/₂ teaspoon dry mustard
1¹/₂ tablespoons cornflour blended with
2 tablespoons water
freshly ground black pepper

1   Cook pasta in boiling water in a
large saucepan following packet
instructions. Drain, set aside and
keep warm.

2   To make sauce, place milk,
stock and mustard in a saucepan
and cook, stirring occasionally, over
a medium heat for 4-5 minutes or
until almost boiling. Stir in cornflour
mixture and cook, stirring
constantly, until sauce boils and
thickens. Season to taste with black
pepper.

3   Add Parmesan and Cheddar
cheeses to sauce and stir until
cheeses melt. Spoon sauce over
pasta and serve immediately.

2030 kilojoules (485 Calories) per serve
Carbohydrate   82.5 g (68%)   *high*
Fat   7 g   *low*

Pasta with Mushroom and Ham Sauce

Serves 4

500 g/1 lb pasta of your choice
MUSHROOM AND HAM SAUCE
300 g/9¹/₂ oz button mushrooms, sliced
4 spring onions, chopped
4 slices reduced-fat-and-salt ham, chopped
¹/₂ cup/125 mL/4 fl oz dry white wine
1 quantity Basic White Sauce (see recipe
this page), heated
freshly ground black pepper

1   Cook pasta in boiling water in a
large saucepan following packet
instructions. Drain, set aside and
keep warm.

2   Place mushrooms, spring onions
and ham in a nonstick frying pan
and cook, stirring, over high heat for
4-5 minutes or until mushrooms are
cooked.

3   Stir in wine, bring to simmering
and simmer for 2 minutes.

4   Stir mushroom mixture into white
sauce and cook, stirring, for 1-2
minutes. Season to taste with black
pepper. Spoon sauce over pasta
and serve immediately.

2050 kilojoules (490 Calories) per serve
Carbohydrate   84 g (69%)   *high*
Fat   4 g   *very low*

REDUCING SALT

▶   Avoid the addition of salt to
food – use herbs and spices for
flavour.
▶   Reduce consumption of salty
foods such as processed meats
and snack foods.
▶   Include some salt-reduced
products in your diet.

Pasta with Mushroom and Ham Sauce, Pasta
with Tomato, Chilli and Herb Sauce, Pasta
with Marinara Sauce, Pasta with Cheese Sauce

Lean Roast

Serves 6

Oven temp: 190°C, 375°F, Gas 5

750 g/1½ lb beef fillet
2 cloves garlic, crushed
2 teaspoons crushed black peppercorns
water

ROAST VEGETABLES
18 large potatoes, halved
6 slices pumpkin
6 pieces sweet potato

GRAVY
2 tablespoons instant gravy powder
½ cup/125 mL/4 fl oz water
½ cup/125 mL/4 fl oz red wine
1 tablespoon Worcestershire sauce

1   To cook vegetables, place potatoes, pumpkin and sweet potato on a nonstick oven tray or a tray lined with nonstick baking paper and bake, turning once, for 1 hour or until vegetables are tender and golden.

2   Rub beef with garlic and black peppercorns and place on a wire rack set in a baking dish. Pour enough water into baking dish to come within 1 cm/½ in of the rack and bake for 40-45 minutes or until beef is cooked to your liking.

3   To make gravy, place instant gravy powder, water, wine and Worcestershire sauce in a small saucepan and cook over a medium heat, stirring constantly, until gravy thickens.

4   To serve, cut meat into slices and serve with roast vegetables, steamed green vegetables and gravy.

Nutrition tip: Add extra potatoes or bread to this meal to boost the carbohydrate. You might like to try Quick Fruit Bread Pudding (page 72) for dessert.

1730 kilojoules (415 Calories) per serve

Carbohydrate	49 g (47%)	low
Fat	6 g	low

Lean Roast

ABSORBING FACTS ABOUT IRON

The amount of iron in food as well as the amount that can be absorbed, from food varies. 'Flesh' foods such as offal (liver and kidneys), red meat, poultry and seafood, contain **haem iron**. This iron is well absorbed by the body. Kidneys, liver and red meat are the richest sources of haem iron.

Plant foods such as bread, breakfast cereal, rice, pasta, fruits and vegetables generally contain less iron than flesh foods. The iron in plant foods is less well absorbed because it is in a **non-haem** form. Dried peas and beans (kidney, baked, soy and the like) are the richest 'vegetarian' sources of iron.

'How do I know if I'm iron deficient?'

Fatigue and lethargy are the early symptoms of iron deficiency anaemia. Dizziness, shortness of breath and palpitations may be experienced if deficiency is severe.

A medical diagnosis of anaemia is made from a blood test which measures haemoglobin, iron stores (ferritin) and a number of other blood components. Iron stores fall first, so they are often used to detect the very early stages of deficiency. Athletic performance may be impaired, even in the early stages of iron deficiency.

'Do I need an iron supplement?'

Iron supplements are required if a blood test confirms iron deficiency. Once iron levels are restored, an improved iron intake will help to prevent deficiency in the future. Iron supplements are a form of medication and should be taken under the supervision of your doctor or dietitian – not on self prescription. Regular blood tests are necessary to determine if there is an adequate response to treatment and then later to detect any subsequent deficiency promptly.

Iron Boosters

Eat:
▶ Meat, chicken or fish daily
▶ Red meat 3 or more times a week
▶ Liver and kidneys regularly

For vegetarians:
▶ Dried peas and beans daily
▶ Vitamin C containing foods with meals
Note:
▶ Vitamin C improves absorption of non-haem iron sources
▶ A factor in meat also improves iron absorption in non-haem iron sources
▶ Vitamin C rich foods include oranges, melons, kiwifruit, red and green peppers

Iron Reducers

Try to avoid the iron-reducers which reduce iron absorption from non-flesh (non-haem) iron sources.

▶ Caffeine in coffee, tea, chocolate, chocolate drinks and cola drinks
▶ Tannin in tea
▶ Phytate found in unprocessed bran

Helpful hints
Try herbal teas or decaffeinated coffee. Reduce the number of cups of caffeine-containing drinks consumed.

Thai Beef

Serves 4

500 g/1 lb rump steak, sliced
1 stalk fresh lemon grass, chopped
or 2 teaspoons finely grated lemon rind
1 teaspoon grated fresh ginger
1 fresh red chilli, finely chopped
1 tablespoon chopped fresh coriander
1 tablespoon lime rind
1 tablespoon lime juice
2 tablespoons desiccated coconut
1/2 cup/125 mL/4 fl oz beef stock
2 teaspoons cornflour blended
with 1 tablespoon water
2 cups/440 g/14 oz rice, cooked

1   Heat a nonstick frying pan over high heat, add beef and stir-fry for 4-5 minutes or until meat is brown.

2   Add lemon grass or lemon rind, ginger, chilli, coriander, lime rind, lime juice, coconut, stock and cornflour mixture and cook, stirring, over a high heat until mixture boils and thickens. Spoon beef mixture over hot rice and serve.

2580 kilojoules (615 Calories) per serve

Carbohydrate	90.5 g (52%)	medium
Fat	10 g	medium

Fruity Pork

Serves 4

500 g/1 lb lean pork, cut into cubes
1 apple, peeled and grated
250 g/8 oz broccoli florets
1 red pepper, chopped
155 g/5 oz green beans, trimmed and halved
45 g/1 1/2 oz chopped dried apricots
1 cup/250 mL/8 fl oz apricot nectar or orange juice
1/2 cup/125 mL/4 fl oz chicken stock
1 tablespoon cornflour blended
with 2 tablespoons water
500 g/1 lb noodles, cooked

1   Heat a nonstick frying pan or wok over a high heat, add pork and stir-fry for 4-5 minutes or until brown and tender.

2   Add apple, broccoli, red pepper, beans and dried apricots to pan and stir-fry for 2-3 minutes or until vegetables are tender crisp.

3   Combine apricot nectar or orange juice, stock and cornflour mixture, add to pan and cook, stirring, for 1 minute or until sauce boils and thickens. Spoon pork mixture over hot noodles and serve immediately.

2815 kilojoules (670 Calories) per serve

Carbohydrate	96 g (57%)	high
Fat	8 g	low

Chilli Chicken Stir-Fry

Serves 4

6 spring onions, finely chopped
4 boneless chicken breast fillets, cut into strips
1 clove garlic, crushed
3 tablespoons sweet chilli sauce
3 tablespoons tomato purée
250 g/8 oz snow peas (mangetout), trimmed
1 red pepper, sliced
2 zucchini (courgettes), sliced
500 g/1 lb pasta, cooked

1   Heat nonstick frying pan or wok over a high heat, add spring onions, chicken and garlic and stir-fry for 3-4 minutes or until chicken is tender.

2   Stir in chilli sauce, tomato purée, snow peas (mangetout), red pepper and zucchini (courgettes) and stir-fry for 2-3 minutes longer or until vegetables are tender crisp. To serve, spoon vegetable mixture over hot pasta.

2185 kilojoules (520 Calories) per serve

Carbohydrate	80 g (61%)	high
Fat	5 g	low

Vegetable Stir-Fry

Serves 4

2 cloves garlic, crushed
2 onions, sliced
1 parsnip, sliced
2 carrots, chopped
2 stalks celery, chopped
1 eggplant (aubergine), finely chopped
8 stalks spinach, shredded
1 red pepper, chopped
250 g/8 oz broccoli florets
3 tablespoons honey
2 tablespoons poppy seeds
500 g/1 lb pasta, cooked

1   Heat a nonstick frying pan or wok over a medium-high heat, add garlic and onions and stir-fry for 2-3 minutes or until onions are soft.

2   Add parsnip, carrots, celery, eggplant (aubergine), spinach, red pepper and broccoli and stir-fry for 3-4 minutes or until vegetables are tender crisp.

3   Stir in honey and poppy seeds and cook for 1 minute longer. Spoon vegetable mixture over hot pasta and serve immediately.

Nutrition tip: To boost carbohydrate, increase the serving size of rice, pasta or noodles.

1990 kilojoules (475 Calories) per serve

Carbohydrate	99 g (83%)	very high
Fat	1.5 g	very low

Curry Lamb Stir-Fry

Serves 4

500 g/1 lb lamb eye loin or lean lamb, trimmed
1 tablespoon mild curry paste
2 onions, sliced into wedges
250 g/8 oz cauliflower florets
1 green pepper, chopped
2 carrots, sliced
1 cup/250 mL/8 fl oz beef stock
1 tablespoon cornflour blended with 1½ tablespoons water
60 g/2 oz sultanas
2 cups/440 g/14 oz rice, cooked

1   Cut lamb into 5 mm/¼ in slices. Heat a nonstick frying pan or wok over a high heat, add lamb and stir-fry for 2-3 minutes or until tender.

2   Remove lamb from pan and set aside. Add curry paste and onions to pan and stir-fry for 2-3 minutes or until onions are soft.

3   Add cauliflower, green pepper and carrots to pan and stir-fry for 2 minutes.

4   Stir beef stock and cornflour mixture into pan and cook, stirring, for 2 minutes or until sauce boils and thickens slightly. Return lamb to pan, add sultanas and cook for 1 minute or until heated through. Spoon lamb mixture over hot rice and serve immediately.

Cook's tip: When stir-frying meat that has been cut into strips or small pieces it is essential to preheat the pan or wok over a high heat before adding the meat. Doing this seals in the juices and the meat will be more tender.

2830 kilojoules (675 Calories) per serve

Carbohydrate	*98 g (57%)*	*high*
Fat	*10 g*	*medium*

Fruity Pork, Curry Lamb Stir-Fry, Thai Beef, Chilli Chicken Stir-Fry, Vegetable Stir-Fry

Vegetable Lasagne

Serves 4
Oven temp: 180°C, 350°F, Gas 4

250 g/8 oz broccoli florets
250 g/8 oz cauliflower florets
125 g/4 oz green beans, sliced
1 red pepper, chopped
2 zucchini (courgettes), sliced
2 carrots, sliced
440 g/14 oz canned tomato purée
2 tablespoons chopped fresh parsley
2 teaspoons chilli sauce
12 sheets instant spinach lasagne
45 g/1¹⁄₂ oz grated Parmesan cheese
45 g/1¹⁄₂ oz grated reduced-fat Cheddar cheese

WHITE SAUCE
2 cups/500 mL/16 fl oz reduced-fat milk
2 tablespoons cornflour blended with 3 tablespoons water
1 teaspoon prepared mild mustard
freshly ground black pepper

1   Heat a large nonstick frying pan over a medium-high heat, add broccoli, cauliflower, beans, red pepper, zucchini (courgettes), carrots, tomato purée, parsley and chilli sauce, bring to simmering and simmer for 6-8 minutes or until vegetables are tender. Remove pan from heat and set aside.

2   To make sauce, place milk in a saucepan and heat over a medium heat, stirring occasionally, for 4-5 minutes or until almost boiling. Stir in cornflour mixture and cook, stirring constantly, for 3-4 minutes or until sauce boils and thickens. Stir in mustard and season to taste with black pepper.

3   Line an ovenproof dish with 4 lasagne sheets, top with one-third of the vegetable mixture, and one-third of the sauce. Repeat layers, finishing with a layer of sauce. Combine Parmesan and Cheddar cheeses, sprinkle over top of lasagne and bake for 30 minutes or until lasagne sheets are soft.

1670 kilojoules (400 Calories) per serve
Carbohydrate   57 g (56%)   high
Fat   9 g   low

Lite Lasagne

Serves 4
Oven temp: 180°C, 350°F, Gas 4

1 onion, chopped
350 g/11 oz lean beef mince
440 g/14 oz canned tomatoes, undrained and mashed
3 tablespoons tomato paste (purée)
¹⁄₂ cup/125 mL/4 fl oz beef stock
freshly ground black pepper
12 sheets instant lasagne
500 g/1 lb low-fat cottage cheese
45 g/1¹⁄₂ oz grated reduced-fat Cheddar cheese

1   Heat a nonstick frying pan over a high heat, add onion and cook for 2-3 minutes or until soft. Stir in beef and cook, stirring frequently, for 4-5 minutes or until well browned.

2   Add tomatoes, tomato paste (purée) and beef stock to pan, bring to simmering and cook, stirring frequently, for 4-5 minutes. Season to taste with black pepper.

3   Line an ovenproof dish with 4 lasagne sheets, top with one-third of the meat mixture and one third of the cottage cheese. Repeat layers finishing with a layer of cottage cheese.

4   Sprinkle top of lasagne with Cheddar cheese and bake for 35-40 minutes or until lasagne sheets are soft.

Serving suggestion: For a complete meal serve lasagne with salad or vegetables and crusty bread.

Nutrition tip: To remove as much fat as possible from mince, after browning remove it from the pan, place on absorbent kitchen paper and allow to drain. Alternatively push the mince to one side of the pan and drain off any fat that has come out during browning. Remember when buying mince to choose the leanest available or buy a lean cut of meat and mince your own.

1645 kilojoules (390 Calories) per serve
Carbohydrate   41 g (28%)   low
Fat   13 g   medium

Spicy Bean Lasagne

Serves 4
Oven temp: 180°C, 350°F, Gas 4

12 sheets instant lasagne
375 g/12 oz low-fat ricotta or cottage cheese
45 g/1¹⁄₂ oz grated reduced-fat mozzarella cheese

SPICY BEANS
1 onion, chopped
1 teaspoon ground cumin
1 teaspoon ground coriander
440 g/14 oz canned red kidney beans, rinsed and drained
440 g/14 oz canned tomatoes, undrained and mashed
2 tablespoons tomato paste (purée)

1   For Spicy Beans, heat a nonstick frying pan over a medium-high heat, add onion and cook, stirring, for 2 minutes or until soft. Stir in cumin and coriander and cook for 1 minute longer.

2   Add beans, tomatoes and tomato paste (purée) to pan, bring to simmering and simmer for 4 minutes or until bean mixture thickens slightly.

3   Line the base of an ovenproof dish with 4 lasagne sheets, top with one-third of the bean mixture and one-third of the ricotta or cottage cheese. Repeat layers finishing with a layer of ricotta or cottage cheese. Sprinkle with mozzarella cheese and bake for 30-35 minutes or until lasagne sheets are soft.

1750 kilojoules (420 Calories) per serve
Carbohydrate   53 g (25%)   low
Fat   12 g   medium

Vegetable Lasagne, Spicy Bean Lasagne, Lite Lasagne

Chicken and Parmesan Risotto

Serves 4

4 cups/1 litre/1³/₄ pt chicken stock
2 cups/500 mL/16 fl oz water
2 cups/440 g/14 oz short-grain rice
90 g/3 oz chopped cooked chicken
2 tablespoons snipped fresh chives
60 g/2 oz grated Parmesan cheese
freshly ground black pepper

1   Place stock and water in a large saucepan and heat over a medium heat until boiling. Place rice in a nonstick frying pan and cook, stirring, over a low heat for 3 minutes.

2   Gradually pour 1 cup/250 mL/8 fl oz stock mixture into rice and cook, stirring, until liquid is absorbed. Repeat this process until all stock mixture is used.

3   Add chicken, chives, Parmesan cheese and black pepper to taste to rice mixture and mix well to combine. Serve immediately.

2035 kilojoules (485 Calories) per serve
Carbohydrate	80 g (65%)	high
Fat	7 g	low

Spiced Rice

Serves 4

2 cups/440 g/14 oz rice
8 cups/2 litres/3¹/₂ pt boiling water
1 cinnamon stick
4 cardamom pods
6 coriander seeds
2 whole cloves
1 tablespoon orange juice
rind 1 orange, cut into strips
rind 1 lemon, cut into strips
60 g/2 oz currants
1 tablespoon chopped fresh coriander

1   Place rice, boiling water, cinnamon stick, cardamom pods, coriander seeds and cloves into a large saucepan, bring to the boil and boil for 10-12 minutes or until rice is tender. Drain rice and remove spices.

2   Place orange juice and orange rind and lemon rind in a saucepan and cook over a low heat for 2 minutes or until soft. Stir in currants, fresh coriander and rice and cook over a medium heat, stirring, for 2 minutes or until heated through. Serve immediately.

2030 kilojoules (485 Calories) per serve
Carbohydrate	109 g (91%)	very high
Fat	0.5 g	very low

Speedy Paella

Serves 4

2 boneless chicken breast fillets, skinned and cut into strips
8 large uncooked prawns, shelled and deveined
4 slices reduced-fat-and-salt ham, sliced
2 cups/440 g/14 oz rice, cooked
pinch ground turmeric
¹/₂ cup/125 mL/4 fl oz chicken stock
60 g/2 oz fresh or frozen peas
2 tablespoons chopped fresh parsley
freshly ground black pepper

1   Heat a nonstick frying pan over a high heat, add chicken and stir-fry for 4-5 minutes or until tender. Remove chicken from pan and set aside.

2   Add prawns to pan and stir-fry for 2-3 minutes or until prawns change colour and are cooked through.

3   Return chicken to pan, add ham, rice, turmeric, stock, peas and parsley and cook, stirring, for 3 minutes or until heated through. Serve immediately. Season to taste with black pepper.

2005 kilojoules (475 Calories) per serve
Carbohydrate	81 g (68%)	high
Fat	4 g	very low

Rice Pie

Serves 4
Oven temp: 180°C, 350°F, Gas 4

2 cups/440 g/14 oz rice, cooked
¹/₂ cup/60 g/2 oz flour
4 egg whites
3 tablespoons tomato paste (purée)
2 tablespoons vegetable stock or water
12 button mushrooms, sliced
1 red pepper, finely chopped
4 spring onions, chopped
1 carrot, grated
2 tablespoons chopped fresh parsley
2 tablespoons sweet chilli sauce (optional)
freshly ground black pepper

1   Place rice, flour, egg whites and tomato paste (purée) in a bowl and mix well to combine.

2   Place stock in a large frying pan and heat over a low heat, add mushrooms, red pepper, spring onions, carrot, parsley, chilli sauce (if using) and black pepper to taste and cook, stirring frequently, for 4-5 minutes or until vegetables are soft.

3   Remove vegetables from pan and set aside to cool slightly. Add vegetable mixture to rice and mix to combine. Spoon rice mixture into a 23 cm/9 in springform tin, lined with nonstick baking paper and bake for 30-40 minutes or until firm.

1895 kilojoules (452 Calories) per serve
Carbohydrate	96 g (85%)	very high
Fat	2 g	very low

Fried Rice

Serves 4

2 eggs, lightly beaten
6 spring onions, chopped
4 slices reduced-fat-and-salt ham, chopped
1 red pepper, chopped
440 g/14 oz canned sweet corn kernels, drained
2 cups/440 g/14 oz rice, cooked
3 tablespoons low-salt soy sauce
2 teaspoons chilli sauce

1   Place eggs and spring onions in a bowl and mix to combine. Heat a nonstick frying pan over a medium heat, pour egg mixture into pan and cook for 2-3 minutes or until set. Remove omelette from pan, roll up, slice and set aside.

2   Wipe pan clean, heat over a medium heat, add ham, red pepper, sweet corn, rice, soy sauce and chilli sauce and stir-fry for 4-5 minutes or until heated through. Add egg strips and toss to combine. Serve immediately.

Microwave it: Cooking rice in the microwave does not save time but it is foolproof and there are no messy saucepans. It is also the perfect way to cook rice for fried rice. To cook rice in the microwave, place 2 cups/440 g/14 oz rice and 4 cups/1 litre/1³/₄ pt water in a large microwave-safe dish and cook, uncovered, on HIGH (100%) for 15-20 minutes or until liquid is absorbed and rice is tender. Fluff up with a fork and use as desired.

2235 kilojoules (535 Calories) per serve
Carbohydrate	102 g (76%)	very high
Fat	5 g	low

Fried Rice, Chicken and Parmesan Risotto, Spiced Rice, Rice Pie, Speedy Paella

White Bowls Pillivuyt   Blue and White Bowl Country Road   Yellow and Blue Bowl Inner City Clayworkers Gallery   Blue and White Plate Lifestyle Imports

Individual Tuna Lasagnes

Serves 4
Oven temp: 180°C, 350°F, Gas 4

16 sheets instant lasagne
60 g/2 oz grated reduced-fat Cheddar cheese

TOMATO TUNA SAUCE
1 onion, chopped
1 clove garlic, crushed
125 g/4 oz broccoli florets
2 zucchini (courgettes), chopped
1 green pepper, chopped
500 mL/16 fl oz jar prepared tomato pasta sauce
440 g/14 oz canned tuna in springwater, drained

CHEESE SAUCE
155 g/5 oz low-fat ricotta cheese
4 tablespoons Parmesan cheese
2-3 tablespoons reduced-fat milk

1   To make Tomato Tuna Sauce, cook onion and garlic in a nonstick frying pan over a medium heat for 2-3 minutes or until onion is soft. Add broccoli, zucchini (courgettes) and green pepper and cook, stirring, for 3-4 minutes or until heated through. Add tomato sauce and tuna and mix to combine. Set aside.

2   To make Cheese Sauce, place ricotta and Parmesan cheeses in a bowl and mix to combine. Stir in enough milk to make a smooth sauce of spreading consistency.

3   Place 1½ sheets of lasagne in a the base of four individual dishes, top with one-quarter of the Tomato Tuna Sauce and 1 tablespoon of the Cheese Sauce. Repeat layers until all ingredients are used. Sprinkle with Cheddar cheese and bake for 30-35 minutes or until lasagne sheets are soft.

Cook's tip: The lasagnes can be cooked in freezerproof containers, frozen and reheated in the microwave. To reheat, first thaw in the refrigerator or defrost in the microwave. Reheat in the oven at 180°C/350°F/Gas 4 for 20 minutes or in the microwave on MEDIUM (50%) for 10 minutes or until heated through.

2715 kilojoules (645 Calories) per serving
Carbohydrate   75 g (45%)   low
Fat   15 g   medium

Cajun Fish and Chips

Serves 4
Oven temp: 200°C, 400°F, Gas 6

4 x 200 g/6½ oz firm white fish fillets
2 tablespoons lemon juice
10 waxy potatoes, cut into wedges

CAJUN SPICE MIX
2 tablespoons sweet paprika
2 teaspoons cracked black pepper
½ teaspoon chilli powder
2 teaspoons ground cumin
2 teaspoons ground oregano
2 teaspoons dried thyme leaves

1   To make spice mix, place paprika, black pepper, chilli powder, cumin, oregano and thyme in a small bowl and mix to combine.

2   Brush fish with lemon juice and roll fish in spice mixture to coat. Set aside.

3   Place potato wedges on a nonstick baking tray, sprinkle with remaining spice mixture and bake for 35-40 minutes or until potatoes are crisp and golden.

4   Preheat a nonstick frying pan over a high heat, add fish and cook for 2 minutes each side or until flesh flakes when tested with a fork. Serve fish with potato wedges.

Serving suggestion: For extra carbohydrate serve with slices of damper.

1330 kilojoules (315 Calories) per serve
Carbohydrate   20 g (25%)   low
Fat   6 g   low

Herb-Crusted Fish

Serves 4
Oven temp: 200°C, 400°F, Gas 6

4 x 200 g/6½ oz firm fish fillets or cutlets

HERB CRUST
2 cups/125 g/4 oz fresh breadcrumbs
2 tablespoons chopped fresh basil
1 teaspoon ground cumin
1 egg white
2 tablespoons lemon juice
crushed black pepper

1   To make crust, place breadcrumbs, basil, cumin, egg white, lemon juice and black pepper to taste in a bowl and mix to combine.

2   Place fish on a foil-lined tray and top each fillet with crust mixture. Bake for 20 minutes or until crust is golden and fish flakes with tested with a fork.

Serving suggestion: Delicious served with spiced potato wedges (see recipe for Cajun Fish and Chips, this page).

1226 kilojoules (272 Calories) per serve
Carbohydrate   15 g (18%)   low
Fat   6 g   low

MELTDOWN MAN

In the Australian summer of 1988 a fit, male runner who was later described by the media as 'meltdown man' went out for an 8 km/5 mile run at 2.30 in the afternoon when the ambient temperature was 38°C/100°F. After collapsing near the end of the run, this man was admitted to hospital where his body (core) temperature was 42°C/107°F. Over the next few months he struggled to stay alive, especially after his muscles began to breakdown or 'meltdown' as the media described it. He needed a ventilator to breathe and a kidney machine. Complications associated with severe dehydration eventually led to one of his legs being amputated. Although this man lived, his story is a reminder of the dangers of exercise in extreme heat and the importance of adequate hydration. For details about keeping cool see page 32.

Herb-Crusted Fish, Individual Tuna Lasagne, Cajun Fish and Chips

Spinach and Barley Pie

Serves 4
Oven temp: 180°C, 350°F, Gas 4

2 cups/440 g/14 oz pearl barley
4 cups/1 litre/1³/₄ pt boiling water
2 tablespoons chopped fresh basil
125 g/4 oz grated pumpkin
2 zucchini (courgettes), grated
1 carrot, grated
1 green pepper, finely chopped
250 g/8 oz packet frozen spinach, thawed, excess water removed
315 g/10 oz canned creamed sweet corn
1 cup/250 g/8 oz low-fat cottage cheese
¹/₂ teaspoon Mexican chilli powder
2 eggs, lightly beaten
4 tablespoons grated reduced-fat Cheddar cheese

1   Place barley in a saucepan, pour over water, cover and cook over a medium heat for 35 minutes or until soft. Drain barley and place in a bowl.

2   Add basil, pumpkin, zucchini (courgettes), carrot, green pepper, spinach, sweet corn, cottage cheese, chilli powder and eggs to barley and mix to combine.

3   Spoon mixture into a large pie dish and sprinkle top of pie with Cheddar cheese. Bake for 35-45 minutes or until pie is firm. Serve hot or cold, cut into wedges.

Cook's tip: For a quicker version of this recipe use quick-cooking barley instead of pearl barley. If using quick-cooking barley the cooking for the barley in step 1 is reduced to 10-15 minutes.

2345 kilojoules (560 Calories) per serve
Carbohydrate   85 g (60%)   high
Fat   9 g   low

Spinach and Barley Pie

Penne with Pumpkin Sauce

Penne with Pumpkin Sauce

Serves 4

500 g/1 lb penne pasta

PUMPKIN SAUCE
500 g/1 lb pumpkin, chopped
2 onions, finely chopped
1 teaspoon ground cumin
$^1/_2$ teaspoon nutmeg
$^1/_2$ teaspoon chilli powder
1 cup/250 mL/8 fl oz reduced-fat milk
2 tablespoons grated Parmesan cheese
freshly ground black pepper

1 Cook pasta in boiling water in a large saucepan following packet instructions. Drain, set aside and keep warm.

2 To make sauce, cook pumpkin in a saucepan of boiling water for 5 minutes or until soft. Drain well and mash.

3 Place onions, cumin, nutmeg and chilli powder in a nonstick frying pan and cook over a medium heat for 4 minutes or until onions are soft. Add pumpkin, stir in milk and cook for 3 minutes or until sauce is heated through. Spoon sauce over pasta and sprinkle with Parmesan cheese and black pepper to taste.

Serving suggestion: For a complete meal serve with crusty bread rolls and a tossed green salad.

2200 kilojoules (525 Calories) per serve
Carbohydrate	*98 g (75%)*	*very high*
Fat	*4 g*	*very low*

Oriental Tofu Stir-Fry

Serves 4

2 tablespoons chopped fresh coriander
2 teaspoons grated fresh ginger
3 tablespoons low-salt soy sauce
2 tablespoons sweet chilli sauce
2 tablespoons plum sauce
375 g/12 oz firm tofu, cut into thick strips
250 g/8 oz snow peas (mangetout), trimmed
1 red pepper, chopped
500 g/1 lb fresh hokkien or rice noodles

1   Place coriander, ginger, soy sauce, chilli sauce and plum sauce in a bowl and mix to combine. Add tofu and toss to coat. Cover and marinate at room temperature for at least 20 minutes.

2   Heat a wok or frying pan over a high heat until hot. Add tofu and stir-fry for 3 minutes. Add snow peas (mangetout) and red pepper and stir-fry for 3 minutes longer. Add noodles and stir-fry for 4 minutes or until noodles are heated through. Serve immediately.

295 kilojoules (70 Calories) per serve

Carbohydrate	42 g (61%)	high
Fat	4.5 g	very low

Thai Noodle Soup

Serves 4

2 tablespoons sweet white miso
4 cups/1 litre/1³/₄ pt water
2 tablespoons fresh coriander leaves
2 spring onions, sliced
2 tablespoons low-salt soy sauce
2 chicken breast fillets, chopped
125 g/4 oz button mushrooms, sliced
125 g/4 oz snow peas (mangetout), sliced
1 carrot, chopped
2 tablespoons lemon or lime juice
2 tablespoons sweet chilli sauce
250 g/8 oz instant Chinese noodles

1   Place miso, water, coriander, spring onions and soy sauce in a saucepan and bring to the boil over a high heat. Reduce heat, add chicken and simmer for 2 minutes.

2   Add mushrooms, snow peas (mangetout), carrot, lemon or lime juice and chilli sauce and cook for 5 minutes. Add noodles and cook for 3 minutes longer or until noodles are soft. Serve in deep bowls.

1280 kilojoules (305 Calories) per serve

Carbohydrate	30 g (61%)	high
Fat	2 g	very low

Spicy Stir-Fried Noodles

Serves 4

1 clove garlic, crushed
3 tablespoons low-salt soy sauce
2 tablespoons oyster sauce
2 tablespoons lime or lemon juice
350 g/11 oz lean rump steak, trimmed of all visible fat and cut into thin slices
2 carrots, chopped
1 green pepper, chopped
125 g/4 oz English spinach leaves
315 g/10 oz fresh hokkien or rice noodles
60 g/2 oz snow pea sprouts or watercress sprigs

1   Place garlic, soy sauce, oyster sauce and lime or lemon juice in a bowl and mix to combine. Add beef, toss to coat, cover and marinate at room temperature for 15 minutes.

2   Drain marinade from beef and reserve. Heat a nonstick frying pan over a high heat, add beef and stir-fry for 3 minutes or until beef just changes colour. Add carrots, green pepper and spinach and stir-fry for 4 minutes. Add noodles and stir-fry for 3 minutes longer or until heated through. Add snow pea sprouts or watercress and toss to combine. Serve immediately.

1010 kilojoules (240 Calories) per serve

Carbohydrate	22 g (35%)	low
Fat	6 g	low

NOODLES

Fresh hokkien and rice noodles are available from Oriental supermarkets or can be found in large supermarkets in the chilled section. As some noodles contain added oil, check the label for fat content when purchasing.

Spicy Stir-Fried Noodles, Oriental Tofu Stir-Fry, Thai Noodle Soup

Spicy Vegetable Couscous

Serves 4
1¹/₂ cups/280 g/9 oz couscous
3 cups/750 mL/1¹/₄ pt boiling water
2 onions, sliced
2 tablespoons sweet chilli sauce
1 teaspoon ground cumin
1 cup/155 g/5 oz canned chickpeas, drained
1 red pepper, chopped
8 spinach leaves, shredded
2 zucchini (courgettes), sliced
¹/₂ cup/125 mL/4 fl oz tomato purée
¹/₂ cup/125 mL/4 fl oz vegetable stock

1   Place couscous in a bowl, pour over boiling water, cover and set aside.

2   Place onions, chilli sauce and cumin in a nonstick frying pan and cook, stirring, over a high heat for 5 minutes or until onions are soft. Add chickpeas, red pepper, spinach and zucchini (courgettes) and stir-fry for 2 minutes.

3   Add tomato purée and stock and cook for 4 minutes longer or until vegetables are soft.

4   To serve, using a fork fluff up couscous to separate grains. Place piles of couscous on serving plates and top with vegetable mixture. Serve with extra sweet chilli sauce.

960 kilojoules (230 Calories) per serve
Carbohydrate   45 g (78%)   very high
Fat   1 g   very low

Spicy Chicken Couscous

For this variation you will need 2 chicken breast fillets, sliced. After cooking the onions add the chicken and stir-fry for 4 minutes or until golden. Complete the recipe as directed.

1218 kilojoules (290 Calories) per serve
Carbohydrate   45 g (61 %)   high
Fat   2.5 g   very low

Couscous with Beef Stir-Fry

Serves 4
1¹/₂ cups/280 g/9 oz couscous
2¹/₂ cups/600 mL/1 pt boiling water
BEEF STIR-FRY
500 g/1 lb rump steak, trimmed of all visible fat, cut into strips
250 g/8 oz green beans, halved
250 g/8 oz broccoli, chopped
4 spring onions, chopped
1 tablespoon chopped fresh coriander
2 tablespoons brown sugar
3 tablespoons low-salt soy sauce
¹/₂ cup/125 mL/4 fl oz beef stock
1 tablespoon tomato paste (purée)
2 teaspoons cornflour blended with 1 tablespoon water

1   Place couscous in a bowl, pour over boiling water, cover and set aside.

2   To make stir-fry, heat a nonstick frying pan over a high heat. Add beef and stir-fry for 5 minutes or until beef is brown. Add beans, broccoli, spring onions, coriander, sugar and soy sauce and stir-fry for 4 minutes.

3   Add stock, tomato paste (purée) and cornflour mixture to pan and cook, stirring, for 3 minutes longer.

4   To serve, using a fork fluff up couscous to separate grains. Place piles of couscous on serving plates and top with Beef Stir-Fry.

1754 kilojoules (418 Calories) per serve
Carbohydrate   45 g (43%)   low
Fat   9.5 g   low

Mediterranean Salad

Serves 4
1¹/₂ cups/375 mL/12 fl oz water
1 cup/250 mL/8 fl oz vegetable stock
1¹/₂ cups/280 g/9 oz couscous
125 g/4 oz young spinach leaves
2 tomatoes, chopped
1 green pepper, chopped
250 g/8 oz chopped cooked lean chicken
2 tablespoons balsamic or red wine vinegar
3 tablespoons currants

1   Place water and stock in a saucepan and bring to the boil. Place couscous in a bowl, pour over boiling stock mixture, cover and set aside to stand for 5 minutes. Using a fork fluff up couscous to separate grains and transfer to a salad bowl.

2   Add spinach, tomatoes, green pepper and chicken to couscous and toss to combine. Sprinkle with vinegar and scatter with currants.

1300 kilojoules (310 Calories) per serve
Carbohydrate   45 g (58%)   high
Fat   4 g   very low

COUSCOUS

Over recent years couscous has become popular as an accompaniment and basis for meals. Couscous is a cracked wheat product made from the endosperm of durum wheat and, like bulghur wheat, is very versatile and quick to prepare. The name refers to both the raw product and the cooked dish. After soaking in water, mix couscous with salad ingredients and serve cold; toss with dried fruits and seeds and nuts and serve as pilau or simply serve with milk and fresh fruit as a breakfast 'porridge'.

Couscous is an excellent source of thiamin as well as being a good source of protein, carbohydrate and niacin.

Couscous with Beef Stir-Fry, Spicy Vegetable Couscous, Mediterranean Salad

FAT
THE HIDDEN OPPONENT

Fat is not always as visible as butter, margarine, the fat on meat, the skin on chicken or the oil we cook in or dress our salads with.

Much of the fat that we eat is hidden inside foods such as cakes, biscuits, confectionery, pies, pastries and fast food. We unknowingly eat more fat than we see. To confuse matters further, fat comes in different types. We need to be aware of which types are best for health and the types that are in different foods.

The Good, the Bad and the Ugly

Triglycerides and cholesterol are two distinctly different fatty type substances in our diet. Triglycerides are such a large and diverse group of fats that they can be classified into three main types:

> *Saturated fat*
> *Mono-unsaturated fat*
> *Polyunsaturated fat*

Of all the fats we eat, research points to the mono-unsaturated and polyunsaturated fats as being the 'good' fats, especially in relation to blood cholesterol levels.

Cholesterol itself is found in foods such as eggs, offal, meat, shellfish, chicken and dairy products. More emphasis is often placed on the cholesterol in foods than the fat, hence the pre-occupation with the label 'Cholesterol Free'. Although eating too much cholesterol is still considered a bad practice, it is the saturated fat in food that increases blood cholesterol levels even more than eating cholesterol itself.

Saturated fat is the 'ugly' dietary fat. Use the 'Finding Fat in Foods' graph opposite to see the amount and type of fat in some popular foods.

FAT-REDUCTION QUIZ

		Yes	No
1	I mostly use reduced-fat dairy products.	☐	☐
2	I always cut the fat off meat.	☐	☐
3	I always remove the skin from chicken.	☐	☐
4	I fry food no more than once a week.	☐	☐
5	I eat high-fat snack foods such as potato crisps, chocolate and french fries, no more than once a week.	☐	☐
6	I spread butter or margarine thinly on bread, or use none at all.	☐	☐
7	If I use oil, I use less than 1 tablespoon for 4 serves. (Tick YES if you don't use oil.)	☐	☐
8	I cook in polyunsaturated or mono-unsaturated oil (olive or canola) instead of butter or dripping. (Tick YES if you don't cook in fat/oil.)	☐	☐
9	I avoid salad dressings or use no-oil varieties.	☐	☐
10	I snack on bread, fruit and cereals in preference to biscuits and cake.	☐	☐
11	I avoid cream.	☐	☐
12	I avoid using butter, margarine or sour cream on vegetables.	☐	☐
	TOTAL		_____

Scoring: For each YES answer SCORE 1 point – the higher your score the better.

FINDING FAT IN FOODS

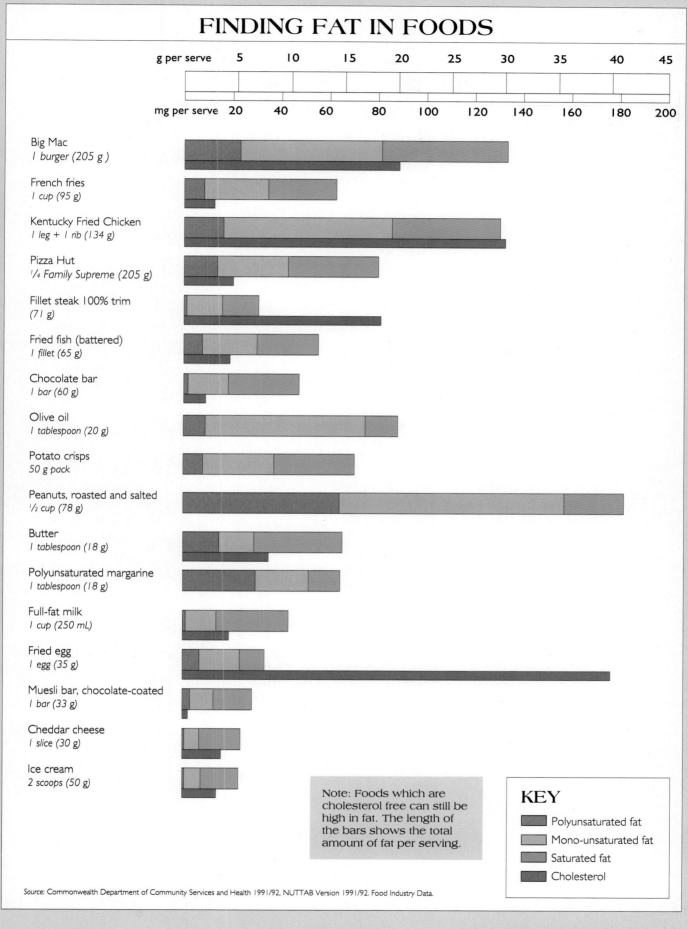

g per serve   5   10   15   20   25   30   35   40   45

mg per serve   20   40   60   80   100   120   140   160   180   200

Big Mac
1 burger (205 g)

French fries
1 cup (95 g)

Kentucky Fried Chicken
1 leg + 1 rib (134 g)

Pizza Hut
¼ Family Supreme (205 g)

Fillet steak 100% trim
(71 g)

Fried fish (battered)
1 fillet (65 g)

Chocolate bar
1 bar (60 g)

Olive oil
1 tablespoon (20 g)

Potato crisps
50 g pack

Peanuts, roasted and salted
½ cup (78 g)

Butter
1 tablespoon (18 g)

Polyunsaturated margarine
1 tablespoon (18 g)

Full-fat milk
1 cup (250 mL)

Fried egg
1 egg (35 g)

Muesli bar, chocolate-coated
1 bar (33 g)

Cheddar cheese
1 slice (30 g)

Ice cream
2 scoops (50 g)

Note: Foods which are cholesterol free can still be high in fat. The length of the bars shows the total amount of fat per serving.

KEY

Polyunsaturated fat
Mono-unsaturated fat
Saturated fat
Cholesterol

Source: Commonwealth Department of Community Services and Health 1991/92, NUTTAB Version 1991/92. Food Industry Data.

FAST FOOD
MADE AT HOME

Herb and Onion Pizzas

Serves 4
Oven temp: 180°C, 350°F, Gas 4

4 x 15 cm/6 in squares focaccia bread

HERB AND ONION TOPPING
2 red onions, sliced
1 onion, sliced
2 cloves garlic, crushed
freshly ground black pepper
1 tablespoon vinegar
3 tablespoons low-oil mayonnaise
2 tablespoons chopped fresh parsley
2 tablespoons chopped fresh basil
90 g/3 oz reduced-fat mozzarella cheese

1   To make topping, heat a nonstick frying pan over a high heat, add red onions and onion and cook, stirring, for 4-5 minutes or until golden. Add garlic and cook for 1 minute longer. Season with black pepper to taste.

2   Stir vinegar into onion mixture. Remove pan from heat and stir in mayonnaise, parsley and basil.

3   Top each focaccia square with one-quarter of the onion mixture. Sprinkle mozzarella cheese over onion mixture and bake for 20 minutes or until cheese is melted and golden.

2570 kilojoules (615 Calories) per serve
Carbohydrate   94 g (58%)   high
Fat   14 g   medium

Sweet and Sour Chicken

Serves 4

4 boneless chicken breast fillets, skinned and cut into strips
6 spring onions, sliced
1 cucumber, chopped
1 green pepper, chopped
155 g/5 oz bean sprouts
440 g/14 oz canned pineapple pieces in natural juice, drained and juice reserved
2 cups/440 g/14 oz rice, cooked

SWEET AND SOUR SAUCE
2 tablespoons tomato sauce
1/4 cup/60 mL/2 fl oz vinegar
1 cup/250 mL/8 fl oz chicken stock
1 1/2 tablespoons cornflour blended with 1 1/2 tablespoons water

1   Heat a nonstick frying pan or wok over a high heat, add chicken strips and stir-fry for 3-4 minutes or until golden and tender.

2   Add spring onions, cucumber, green pepper and bean sprouts and stir-fry for 2 minutes.

3   To make sauce, combine tomato sauce, vinegar, stock, cornflour mixture and reserved pineapple juice. Stir sauce and pineapple pieces into chicken mixture and cook, stirring, for 2-3 minutes or until sauce boils and thickens. Serve with hot rice.

2500 kilojoules (595 Calories) per serve
Carbohydrate   105 g (70%)   very high
Fat   4.5 g   very low

Hamburgers

Serves 4

4 hamburger buns, split and toasted
8 lettuce leaves
8 slices tomato
8 slices beetroot
4 slices reduced-fat Cheddar cheese

MEAT PATTIES
350 g/11 oz lean beef mince
1 cup/60 g/2 oz breadcrumbs, made from stale bread
1 egg, lightly beaten
2 tablespoons Worcestershire sauce
freshly ground black pepper

1   To make patties place beef, breadcrumbs, egg, Worcestershire sauce and black pepper to taste in a bowl and mix well to combine.

2   Divide meat mixture into four portions and shape into patties. Heat a nonstick frying pan over a medium heat and cook patties for 4-5 minutes each side or until cooked to your liking.

3   Top bottom half of each bun with a pattie, 2 lettuce leaves, 2 slices tomato, 2 slices beetroot and 1 slice cheese and top half of bun. Serve immediately.

1915 kilojoules (455 Calories) per serve
Carbohydrate   40 g (35%)   low
Fat   17 g   high

Herb and Onion Pizzas, Hamburgers, Sweet and Sour Chicken

Pan Basic Essentials

Fat and alcohol are your biggest threats when you eat out. The following strategies will help you to head off the 'overdone it' hangover, yet still have a great time.

▶ Ask for plain bread (no butter). Avoid garlic and herb bread, which is usually soaked in butter.

▶ Watch out for dressings and creamy or cheese sauces which are sometimes added – order a brown or tomato-based sauce instead.

▶ Choose barbecued or grilled rather than pan-fried or deep-fried foods.

▶ Trim the fat off meat and take the skin off chicken. Watch out for French fries – instead order plain vegetables or salad (without dressing if possible).

▶ Ask for your food to be cooked in a low-fat way. You will find that most restaurants try their best to help you.

▶ Order a jug of water for your table – you will drink less alcohol and keep yourself better hydrated.

▶ Skip the pre-dinner drinks. Plan to have only 1 or 2 alcoholic drinks with the meal.

▶ Order less food. One or two courses should be ample. Alternatively, you can order two first courses and cut down that way.

▶ Try a vegetable soup or salad for the first course.

▶ Ask what accompaniments come with the main course – you can then avoid being tempted by chips, buttered vegetables and the like. Ask for lower fat alternatives when you order.

▶ Order extra bread instead of chips.

Pitta Pizzas

Serves 4
Oven temp: 180°C, 350°F, Gas 4

4 small pitta bread rounds

PIZZA TOPPING
¹/₂ cup/125 mL/4 fl oz prepared tomato pasta sauce or tomato paste (purée)
1 small red pepper, sliced
250 g/8 oz canned pineapple pieces, drained
2 slices reduced-fat-and-salt ham, cut into strips
8 button mushrooms, sliced
90 g/3 oz grated reduced-fat Cheddar cheese

1 Place bread rounds on nonstick baking trays and spread each with tomato sauce or paste (purée).

2 Top bread rounds with red pepper, pineapple, ham, mushrooms and cheese and bake for 15-20 minutes or until pizzas are crisp and cheese is melted and golden.

1110 kilojoules (265 Calories) per serve

Carbohydrate	34 g (50%)	medium
Fat	7.5 g	low

Chicken Pizzas

Serves 4
Oven temp: 180°C, 350°F, Gas 4

4 x 15 cm/6 in squares focaccia bread

CHICKEN TOPPING
¹/₂ cup/125 mL/4 fl oz prepared tomato pasta sauce
90 g/3 oz chopped cooked chicken
8 mushrooms, chopped
1 green pepper, chopped
4 spring onions, finely chopped
4 pitted black olives, sliced
60 g/2 oz grated reduced-fat Cheddar cheese
30 g/1 oz grated Parmesan cheese

1 Spread each square of focaccia with tomato sauce. Top with chicken, mushrooms, green pepper, spring onions and olives. Combine Cheddar and Parmesan cheeses and sprinkle over chicken and vegetables.

2 Place pizzas on nonstick baking trays and bake for 20 minutes or until cheese is melted and golden brown.

2715 kilojoules (645 Calories) per serve

Carbohydrate	96 g (56%)	high
Fat	15 g	medium

Pitta Pizzas, Chicken Pizzas

Pork with Plum Sauce

Serves 4

500 g/1 lb pork fillet, trimmed of all visible fat
6 spring onions, sliced
2 zucchini (courgettes), sliced
1 red pepper, chopped
2 stalks celery, chopped
250 g/8 oz broccoli florets
freshly ground black pepper
2 cups/440 g/14 oz rice or 500 g/1 lb noodles, cooked

PLUM SAUCE
2 tablespoons low-salt soy sauce
4 tablespoons plum jam
1/2 cup/125 mL/4 fl oz chicken stock
3 teaspoons cornflour blended with 1 tablespoon water

1   Cut pork into thin medallions. Heat a large nonstick frying pan or wok over a high heat, add pork and stir-fry for 4-5 minutes or until browned.

2   Add spring onions, zucchini (courgettes), red pepper, celery and broccoli and stir-fry for 3-4 minutes longer.

3   To make sauce, place soy sauce, jam, stock and cornflour mixture in a small bowl and mix to combine. Stir sauce into pork mixture and cook, stirring, for 2-3 minutes or until heated through. Season to taste with black pepper and serve with hot rice or noodles.

2810 kilojoules (670 Calories) per serve
Carbohydrate   102.5 g (60%)   high
Fat   7.5 g   low

Sesame Beef

Serves 4

500 g/1 lb rump steak, trimmed of all visible fat and cut into strips
3 tablespoons low-salt soy sauce
2 tablespoons honey
1 clove garlic, crushed
1 tablespoon sesame seeds
2 onions, sliced
1 red pepper, sliced
200 g/6 1/2 oz snow peas (mangetout), trimmed
155 g/5 oz button mushrooms, sliced
2 cups/440 g/14 oz rice or 500 g/1 lb noodles, cooked

1   Place meat, soy sauce, honey, garlic and sesame seeds in a bowl, cover and set aside to marinate for 30 minutes.

2   Drain meat and reserve marinade. Heat a nonstick frying pan or wok over a high heat, add meat and stir-fry for 2-3 minutes. Remove meat from pan, set aside and keep warm.

3   Add onions to pan and stir-fry for 2-3 minutes or until tender. Add red pepper, snow peas (mangetout) and mushrooms and stir-fry for 2 minutes longer. Return meat to pan, stir in reserved marinade and cook for 1 minute. Serve with hot rice or noodles.

2920 kilojoules (695 Calories) per serve
Carbohydrate   95 g (54%)   medium
Fat   11 g   medium

Mongolian Lamb

Serves 4

500 g/1 lb lamb fillets, trimmed of all visible fat
2 onions, chopped
2 cups/440 g/14 oz rice or 500 g/1 lb noodles, cooked

GINGER CHILLI SAUCE
2 tablespoons low-salt soy sauce
1 clove garlic, crushed
1 teaspoon grated fresh ginger
1/2 cup/125 mL/4 fl oz red wine
2 tablespoons sweet chilli sauce

1   Cut lamb into thin medallions.

2   Heat a nonstick frying pan or wok over a medium-high heat, add onions and stir-fry for 3-4 minutes or until golden.

3   Add lamb to pan and stir-fry for 4-5 minutes or until tender.

4   To make sauce, place soy sauce, garlic, ginger, wine and chilli sauce in a bowl and mix to combine. Add sauce to pan and cook, stirring, for 3-4 minutes or until sauce thickens. Serve with hot rice or noodles.

2755 kilojoules (655 Calories) per serve
Carbohydrate   90 g (54%)   medium
Fat   9.5 g   low

Sesame Beef, Mongolian Lamb, Pork with Plum Sauce

Plates In Residence   Cutlery Orrefors Kosta Boda

Spicy Chicken Burgers

Serves 4

1 teaspoon ground cumin
1 teaspoon ground coriander
1 teaspoon paprika
1/4 teaspoon chilli powder
4 boneless chicken breast fillets, skinned
4 rolls, split and lightly toasted
8 lettuce leaves
4 tablespoons low-oil mayonnaise
1/2 avocado, stoned, peeled and chopped

1   Place cumin, coriander, paprika and chilli powder in a bowl and mix to combine. Add chicken to spice mixture and toss to coat.

2   Heat a nonstick frying pan over a high heat, add chicken and cook for 3-4 minutes each side or until tender and cooked through.

3   Top bottom half of each bun with a chicken fillet, 2 lettuce leaves, 1 tablespoon mayonnaise, some of the avocado and top half of bun. Serve immediately.

1300 kilojoules (310 Calories) per serve

Carbohydrate	22 g (28%)	low
Fat	12 g	medium

Steak Sandwiches

Serves 4

4 small pieces rump steak, trimmed of all visible fat
2 onions, sliced
8 thick slices bread, toasted
4 tablespoons barbecue sauce
4 slices reduced-fat Cheddar cheese

1   Heat a nonstick frying pan over a high heat, add steak and cook for 3-4 minutes each side or until cooked to your liking. Remove steak from pan, set aside and keep warm.

2   Add onions to pan and cook, stirring, for 4-5 minutes or until golden and soft.

3   Divide the steak and onions between half the bread slices then top each with 1 tablespoon barbecue sauce, 1 slice cheese and finally a slice of the remaining bread. Serve immediately.

Serving suggestion: Serve Steak Sandwiches with a salad for a complete meal.

1235 kilojoules (295 Calories) per serve

Carbohydrate	35 g (46%)	low
Fat	8 g	low

Soya Burgers

Serves 4

4 rolls, split and toasted
1 carrot, grated
4 slices tomato
1 raw beetroot, peeled and grated (optional)
2-3 tablespoons sweet chilli sauce

SOYA PATTIES
440 g/14 oz canned soya beans, rinsed and drained
125 g/4 oz low-fat cottage cheese
1 cup/60 g/ 2 oz breadcrumbs, made from stale bread
1 teaspoon ground cumin

1   To make patties, place half the soya beans in a bowl and mash with a fork. Add remaining beans, cottage cheese, breadcrumbs and cumin and mix well to combine. Divide bean mixture into four portions and shape into patties.

2   Heat a nonstick frying pan over a medium heat, add patties and cook for 4-6 minutes each side or until brown and heated through.

3   Top bottom half of each roll with a pattie, some carrot, a tomato slice, some beetroot (if using), chilli sauce to taste and top half of roll. Serve immediately.

1355 kilojoules (325 Calories) per serve

Carbohydrate	39 g (47%)	low
Fat	8 g	low

Fish Burgers

Serves 4

4 x 100 g/3 1/2 oz firm white fish fillets
3 tablespoons water
1 tablespoon lemon juice
6 black peppercorns
2 sprigs fresh dill
4 rolls, split and toasted

TARTARE SAUCE
1/2 cup/125 mL/4 fl oz low-oil mayonnaise
2 gherkins, chopped
2 teaspoons chopped fresh dill
freshly ground black pepper

1   To make sauce, place mayonnaise, gherkins, dill and black pepper to taste in a bowl and mix to combine.

2   Place fish, water, lemon juice, peppercorns and dill in a large nonstick frying pan, bring to simmering over a low heat and simmer, turning once, for 3-4 minutes or until fish flakes when tested with a fork. Remove fish from liquid.

3   Top bottom half of each roll with a fish fillet, 1 tablespoon sauce and top half of roll. Serve immediately.

1025 kilojoules (245 Calories) per serve

Carbohydrate	22 g (35%)	low
Fat	4 g	very low

Fish Burger, Soya Burger,
Steak Sandwich, Spicy Chicken Burger

CAN YOU KICK THE SALT HABIT?

Salt (sodium chloride) is the main source of sodium in our diet. In countries where salt intake is high, there is an increased rate of high blood pressure, stroke and heart disease.

The body's requirements for salt are low – a mere 0.5 g/day is all that we need. In Western countries the average daily intake is about ten times this amount. Of the salt we eat, 75% comes from processed foods, 15-20% from the salt we add to food and only about 10% from fresh foods such as milk, meat, seafood and fruit.

Sweating increases our salt loss, but the body adapts to reduce the salt content in sweat (and in urine) when large amounts of sweat are lost on a regular basis. Therefore eating extra salt is not necessary, even for those athletes who sweat heavily.

In longer or ultra-endurance events (greater than 4 hours strenuous, uninterrrupted effort) the body could need extra salt. Large sweat losses occurring in these events increase the chance of blood sodium levels falling, particularly if lots of plain water is used to replace sweat losses. Sodium (salt) losses are best replaced during the event with the help of a fluid-replacement drink containing a low concentration of salt (sodium). There is no need for these athletes to consume extra salt at other times. Salt tablets are not recommended as they may upset the stomach.

EATING TO WIN

COMPETITION EATING

Your dietary needs for competition are dictated by the type of sport you participate in. Read through this guide to competition eating so you will be eating to win.

On Your Mark

Carbohydrate (glycogen) loading

Carbohydrate loading increases the body's store of glycogen. The extra glycogen is loaded to ensure an adequate supply of glycogen for endurance exercise, where normal stores will not be sufficient to maintain stamina. 'Hitting the wall' is an expression used by endurance athletes to describe the feeling they get when glycogen stores are almost exhausted. The 'wall' is a wall of fatigue they feel they cannot pass through.

Earliest loading methods included a glycogen depletion phase. The depletion phase, employed to make the muscles 'hungrier for glycogen' was achieved by strenuous, endurance exercise and severe restriction of carbohydrate intake. Consequently, athletes felt tired, irritable and had difficulty in maintaining motivation and concentration. After 2-3 days of depletion, glycogen was loaded through a diet rich in carbohydrate (9-10 g carbohydrate/kg body weight/day or 80-85% of energy from carbohydrate).

In the 1980s a modified loading method was developed. This method simply involved tapered (reduced) training and a high-carbohydrate diet. The depletion phase was omitted, as similar amounts of glycogen could be loaded without it and the side effects associated with this phase were eliminated.

This modified method is now the only loading method recommended.

Who needs carbohydrate loading?

Carbohydrate loading is only useful for endurance athletes competing in events longer than 90 minutes. In shorter events, an adequate, rather than 'loaded', glycogen store is appropriate. This can be achieved by tapering training and ensuring a high carbohydrate intake (9-10 g carbohydrate/kg body weight/day) 24-36 hours prior to competition.

Low blood sugar (hypoglycaemia)

Endurance exercise places huge demands on the body's carbohydrate reserves. As a result, blood sugar levels may fall too low. Dizziness, shakiness, faintness and confusion are symptoms of hypoglycaemia, or low blood sugar. Athletes may refer to this as 'bonking'.

Adequate preparation for endurance events through carbohydrate loading and replacement of carbohydrate during the event with sports drinks (5-10% carbohydrate) or food snacks help to prevent this problem.

Loading tips

▶ Taper (reduce) training to decrease the use of muscle glycogen. This is also important to help you peak. Rest on the day prior to competition. Cramming in extra training this close to competiton does more harm than good.

▶ Eat extra carbohydrate for 3-4 days prior to the event. Aim to consume about 9-10 g of carbohydrate/kg of body weight/day (page 19).

▶ If feeling full or bloated, try reducing fibre intake. Choose white bread, rice or pasta and more refined cereals such as Cornflakes or Rice Bubbles, instead of the higher fibre, wholegrain ones. Resume a high-fibre diet after competition.

▶ If you can't manage to eat the amount of food you need, juices, soft drinks and high-carbohydrate sports drinks help to supplement food intake.

▶ Check your body weight. Approximately 3 g of water are stored with each gram of loaded glycogen. Expect to gain about 2 kg/ 4 lb. The water stored assists hydration during the event.

Get Set

Precompetition meal

Your precompetition meal has the potential to either make or break your performance on the day. What you will be eating should not be left to chance. Work on a dietary strategy using the following guidelines, then practise this strategy before a training session so you can fine-tune your diet.

There is some evidence that foods with a low glycaemic index are best prior to endurance events. Pasta and porridge have a low glycaemic index and are often favourites of athletes prior to competition. You need to experiment with the low glycaemic index strategy prior to competition to find out if it works for you.

PRECOMPETITION MEAL GUIDELINES

▶ High in carbohydrate – for maximum energy

▶ Low in fat – fat slows digestion

▶ Moderate protein – fill up on carbohydrates instead

▶ Avoid salty foods and added salt – salt (and excess protein) has a diuretic (dehydrating) effect

▶ Avoid caffeine and alcohol – they have a diuretic effect

▶ Moderate fibre – not too much of a good thing (see page 29)

▶ Top up, don't pig out – eat a comfortable amount of food

▶ Drink your meal – if you're too nervous, or you feel it's too early in the morning to eat, try a sports drink, or see drinks recipes (page 31). Maintain your energy with liquid food

▶ Practise – experiment with different meals to find out which foods work best for you

The Precompetition Meal

There is no perfect precompetition meal. Use these guidelines to develop your own precompetition meal plan, based around the foods you enjoy.

GOOD BREAKFAST
Wholegrain cereal with reduced-fat milk
Fresh fruit
2 slices toast spread with jam (no butter or margarine)
1 glass pure fruit juice (100%)

Nutritional Analysis
Energy	2100 kJ (500 Cal)	
Protein	12 g (10%)	
Fat	4 g (5 %)	
Carbohydrate	100 g (85%)	

▶ Cereal, bread, fruit and fruit juice are high in carbohydrate and low in fat.
▶ To lower the glycaemic index try porridge and bread containing barley or oats.

NOT RECOMMENDED BREAKFAST
1 fried egg
2 rashers bacon with fat
1 beef sausage
2 thick slices white toast spread thickly with butter
1 cup black coffee, no sugar

Nutritional Analysis
Energy	2100 kJ (500 Cal)	
Protein	30 g (23%)	
Fat	33 g (50%)	
Carbohydrate	30 g (27%)	

▶ The egg, bacon and sausage fry-up is high in fat.
▶ The meal is low in carbohydrate.
▶ The caffeine in the coffee has a diuretic (dehydrating) effect.

GOOD DINNER
White spaghetti, topped with tomato-based sauce (prepared without fat or oil)
1 large white bread roll (no butter or margarine)
Fresh fruit
1 glass orange juice (100%)

Nutritional Analysis
Energy	4300 kJ (1000 Cal)	
Protein	33 g (14%)	
Fat	7 g (6%)	
Carbohydrate	200 g (80%)	

▶ Pasta, bread, fruit and fruit juice are all low in fat and high in carbohydrate.
▶ Small amounts of meat, fish or chicken can be added to the sauce if desired.
▶ To lower the glycaemic index try bread containing barley or oats..

NOT RECOMMENDED DINNER
Rump steak fried with fat
1 baked jacket potato
Green salad
Garlic bread, spread thickly with butter
2 scoops vanilla ice cream

Nutritional Analysis
Energy	4240 kJ (1000 Cal)	
Protein	71 g (29%)	
Fat	57 g (50%)	
Carbohydrate	55 g (21%)	

▶ Carbohydrate content is too low.
▶ Fat on meat, in garlic butter on bread and in ice cream results in a meal too high in fat.

Precompetition proportions

You should aim for the following when planning your precompetition meal.
Fat – less than 20% of energy (less than 10 g fat/meal)
Carbohydrate – about 80-85% of energy
Compare the precompetition 'good' and 'not recommended' breakfasts and dinners and see how they rate.

The meal immediately prior to the event, the precompetition meal, is like the 'icing on the cake'. This one meal can't work miracles if the diet leading up to competition has been inadequate. However, this one meal could break your performance if the wrong foods are eaten.

'When should I eat my precompetition meal?'

You will feel more comfortable if you eat your precompetition meal 2-4 hours prior to the event. This allows time for the meal to be emptied from the stomach. Allow 4 hours for a larger meal.

'I compete in a series of heats/ sessions throughout the day. What should I eat in between?'

Eat small amounts regularly throughout the day. You will feel more comfortable if you are not over full. In shorter breaks (less than 1 hour) drinks are best; try either water or a fluid-replacement drink. In longer breaks, try a light snack (see box above) or a fruit drink or reduced-fat milk drink. Refuelling with a drink between events aids rehydration and is often more comfortable and convenient than food.

'If I eat well the evening before the event, do I still need to eat breakfast?'

Yes, you do! Liver glycogen stores fall overnight. While you sleep, your liver uses its stores of glycogen to top up blood sugar levels. If these stores are not replaced prior to the event, your concentration levels may slide, you may even feel dizzy or sleepy during competition. To compete at your maximum, both liver and muscle glycogen stores need to be at their best. Fruit sugar, fructose, is taken up quickly by the liver so it's good to include some fruit or juice in your precompetition breakfast. A homemade (see page 31) or commercially available liquid meal, such as Exceed Sports Meal or Sustagen Sport, is fine if eating solid food prior to the event is difficult for you.

MEAL IDEAS

Pre-event
▶ Breakfast cereal with reduced-fat milk and fresh, canned or dried fruit

▶ Pancakes with honey, jam or maple syrup

▶ English muffins, crumpets or bread/toast topped with jam, honey, banana, baked beans or spaghetti

▶ Pasta with tomato or low-fat sauce

▶ Homemade liquid meals (page 31) or commercial varieties, such as Exceed Sports Meal or Sustagen

Between Events
As for pre-event, plus:

◗ Quick Banana Rice Custard (page 14). This is delicious cold

◗ Cheese and Chive Scones (page 11)

◗ Muffins (page 11)

◗ Muesli Bars (page 11)

◗ Pikelets (page 14)

◗ Banana sandwich

◗ Honey or jam sandwich

◗ Fruit Bread Pudding (page 72)

◗ Sandwiches

◗ Power bars

◗ Low-fat yogurt

◗ Fresh, canned or dried fruit

'I get a bloated or upset stomach if I eat before I compete – what foods should I try?'

Use the ideas and guidelines on this page and on page 66 as a starting point. If you get no relief, try a liquid meal as these are well tolerated even by those who have a 'nervous' or sensitive stomach, prior to an event. Liquid meals are also low in fibre so they help to prevent excessive bowel movement before or during the event. See also 'Fibre – too much of a good thing?' (page 29).

Go

During the event, fluid replacement is vital for everyone. Refuelling with carbohydrate along the way will benefit endurance athletes, particularly if the events are longer than 2 hours. See the section on fluids and refuelling (page 32). Don't forget your recovery strategies after the event (see page 19).

3-DAY PRECOMPETITON MENU PLAN

Menu plan explained

Each daily menu provides approximately 14 700 kilojoules (3500 Calories). Of this, 10 500 kilojoules (3000 Calories) comes from meals and the remainder from snacks. The energy (kilojoule/calorie) level is suitable for active males. For females and those less active, smaller servings and reducing or omitting some of the snacks will help to decrease the energy to the appropriate level. Alternatively, increasing foods such as bread, fruit, juice, rice and pasta will increase the energy and carbohydrate in the daily menu.

The proportion of energy from protein, fat and carbohydrate is approximately 20% protein, 10% fat and 70% carbohydrate. This plan will give you ideas on how to organise your own high-carbohydrate, low-fat menu plans using other foods and recipes from this book.

DAY 1

BREAKFAST
1 piece fresh fruit
Banana Porridge (page 7) with reduced-fat milk
2 slices bread or toast spread with jam, honey or marmalade
1 small glass fruit juice

MORNING SNACK
Mango Smoothie (page 31)

LUNCH
3 sandwiches or bread rolls (see page 22 for Delicious Sandwich Fillings)
2 pieces fresh fruit
1 small glass fruit juice

AFTERNOON SNACK
Honey Soy Noodles (page 12)

DINNER
Curry Lamb Stir-Fry (page 43) served with rice and either steamed vegetables or a salad (no-oil dressing)
2 pieces fresh fruit
1 small glass fruit juice

SUPPER
1 piece fresh fruit
2 slices raisin bread spread with jam, honey or marmalade
1 small glass fruit juice

DAY 2

BREAKFAST
1 piece fresh fruit
1 large bowl Kellogg's Sustain with reduced-fat milk
2 slices bread or toast spread with jam, honey or marmalade
1 glass reduced-fat milk

MORNING SNACK
1 piece fresh fruit

LUNCH
Spinach and Pasta Salad (page 20)
1 piece fresh fruit
1 small glass fruit juice

AFTERNOON SNACK
1 Banana Muffin (page 11)
1 small glass fruit juice

DINNER
Pork with Plum Sauce (page 62) served with rice or noodles and extra steamed vegetables or a salad (no-oil dressing)
2 slices bread or a bread roll
1 piece fresh fruit
1 Pineapple Crush (page 31)

SUPPER
2 crumpets spread with jam or honey
1 small glass reduced-fat milk

DAY 3

BREAKFAST
3 pieces fresh fruit, chopped and served with 1 carton (200 g/6½ oz) low-fat fruit yogurt
2 Pancakes (page 76)
1 small glass fruit juice

MORNING SNACK
1 Muesli Bar (page 11)
1 small glass fruit juice

LUNCH
1 Chicken Satay Roll-Up (page 24)
1 piece fresh fruit
1 Powershake (page 31)

AFTERNOON SNACK
1 piece fresh fruit
1 small glass fruit juice

DINNER
Pasta with Tomato, Chilli and Herb Sauce (page 38)
2 slices bread or a bread roll
Quick Fruit Bread Pudding (page 72)
1 small glass fruit juice

SUPPER
1 large bowl wholegrain cereal with reduced-fat milk
1 piece fresh fruit

SWEET TREATS
SPECIAL REWARDS

Carrot Cake with Lemon Frosting

Serves 12
Oven temp: 180°C, 350°F, Gas 4

1 cup/125 g/4 oz flour
1 teaspoon baking powder
¹/₂ teaspoon bicarbonate of soda
³/₄ cup/125 g/4 oz brown sugar
1 carrot, grated
¹/₂ cup/90 g/3 oz chopped canned
pineapple, drained
2 eggs
2 tablespoons vegetable oil
1 teaspoon ground cinnamon

LEMON FROSTING
125 g/4 oz low-fat ricotta cheese
¹/₄ cup/45 g/1¹/₂ oz icing sugar
1 tablespoon lemon juice

1   Sift together flour, baking powder
and bicarbonate of soda into a
bowl, add sugar and mix to
combine.

2   Add carrot, pineapple, eggs, oil
and cinnamon and mix well.

3   Spoon batter into an 18 cm/7 in
round cake tin lined with nonstick
baking paper and bake for 35-40
minutes or until cooked when tested
with a skewer. Allow cake to stand
in tin for 5 minutes before turning
onto a wire rack to cool completely.

4   To make frosting, place ricotta
cheese, icing sugar and lemon juice
in a food processor and process
until smooth. Spread over the top of
cold cake.

625 kilojoules (150 Calories) per slice

Carbohydrate	23 g (60%)	high
Fat	5 g	low

Chocolate Brownies

Makes 16 squares
Oven temp: 180°C, 350°F, Gas 4

³/₄ cup/90 g/3 oz flour
¹/₂ teaspoon baking powder
¹/₂ cup/45 g/1¹/₂ oz cocoa powder
1 cup/ 220 g/7 oz caster sugar
¹/₂ cup/100 g/3 oz low-fat vanilla yogurt
2 eggs
1 teaspoon vanilla essence
1¹/₂ tablespoons vegetable oil

1   Sift together flour, baking powder
and cocoa powder into a bowl. Add
sugar, yogurt, eggs, vanilla essence
and oil and mix to combine.

2   Spoon batter into a 20 cm/8 in
square cake tin lined with nonstick
baking paper and bake for 25-30
minutes. Allow brownies to cool in
tin before turning out and cutting
into squares.

Cook's tip: If you do not have a
nonstick baking tin, line tin with
nonstick baking paper.

500 kilojoules (120 Calories) per brownie

Carbohydrate	21 g (68%)	high
Fat	3 g	very low

Carrot Cake with Lemon Frosting, Brownies

Quick Fruit Bread Pudding

Serves 6
Oven temp: 180°C, 350°F, Gas 4

8 slices fruit bread
2 tablespoons jam
3 eggs
2¹/₂ cups/600 mL/I pt skim milk

1   Trim crusts from bread and cut slices into triangles. Spread each triangle with a little jam and arrange in a 6 cup/1.5 litre/2¹/₂ pt capacity ovenproof dish.

2   Place eggs and milk in a bowl and whisk to combine. Pour milk mixture over bread and bake for 35-40 minutes or until custard is set and top is golden.

Serving suggestion: This dessert is delicious served with low-fat ice cream or low-fat vanilla yogurt.

845 kilojoules (200 Calories) per serve
Carbohydrate   31.5 g (61%)   high
Fat   4 g   very low

Fruit with Strawberry Dip

Serves 4

200 g/6¹/₂ oz vanilla *fromage frais*
200 g/6¹/₂ oz strawberries
fresh fruit of your choice

Place strawberries in a food processor or blender and process to make a purée. Place strawberry purée in a bowl, add *fromage frais* and mix to combine. Serve with fruit.

225 kilojoules (55 Calories) per serve of dip
Carbohydrate   7.5 g (55%)   medium
Fat   I g   very low

Mango Cheesecake

Serves 12
Oven temp: 180°C, 350°F, Gas 4
BASE
8 Weet-Bix (Weetabix), crushed
2 tablespoons honey
2 tablespoons orange juice
MANGO FILLING
1½ cups/300 g/10 oz low-fat vanilla yogurt
500 g/1 lb low-fat ricotta cheese
¼ cup/60 mL/2 fl oz lemon juice
½ cup/100 g/3½ oz caster sugar
4 egg whites
2 x 440 g/14 oz canned mango slices,
drained

1   To make base, place Weet-Bix
(Weetabix), honey and orange juice
in a bowl and mix well to combine.
Press base into a 23 cm/9 in
springform tin lined with nonstick
baking paper and bake for 10
minutes.

2   To make filling, place yogurt,
ricotta cheese, lemon juice, sugar,
egg whites and half the mango
slices in a food processor and
process until smooth. Roughly chop
remaining mango slices and fold
into filling.

3   Spoon filling over base and bake
for 35-45 minutes or until set.
Refrigerate until well chilled before
serving.

830 kilojoules (200 Calories) per serve

Carbohydrate	33 g (65%)	high
Fat	4 g	very low

Mango Cheesecake, Quick Fruit Bread
Pudding, Fruit with Strawberry Dip

Pumpkin Fruit Cake

Serves 12
Oven temp: 180°C, 350°F, Gas 4

¹/₂ cup/60 g/2 oz self-raising flour
1 cup/125 g/4 oz flour
¹/₂ cup/125 g/4 oz demerara sugar
155 g/5 oz mixed dried fruit
1 cup/250 g/8 oz cooked mashed pumpkin
1 egg
¹/₂ cup/100 g/3¹/₂ oz low-fat natural yogurt
1 teaspoon vanilla essence

1   Sift together self-raising flour and flour in a bowl, add sugar and dried fruit and mix to combine.

2   Make a well in the centre of the flour mixture, add pumpkin, egg, yogurt and vanilla essence and mix to combine.

3   Spoon batter into a 20 cm/8 in square cake tin lined with nonstick baking paper and bake for 50-60 minutes or until cake is cooked when tested with a skewer.

615 kilojoules (145 Calories) per slice
Carbohydrate	32 g (85%)	very high
Fat	1 g	very low

Apricot Bran Loaf

Serves 12
Oven temp: 180°C, 350°F, Gas 4

60 g/2 oz chopped dried apricots
¹/₄ cup/60 mL/2 fl oz hot water
¹/₂ cup/75 g/2¹/₂ oz wholemeal flour
1 cup/125 g/4 oz self-raising flour
1 teaspoon baking powder
1 cup/100 g/3¹/₂ oz bran cereal
2 eggs
¹/₄ cup/45 g/1¹/₂ oz low-fat natural yogurt
¹/₂ cup/170 g/5¹/₂ oz honey
1 teaspoon ground allspice

1   Place apricots in a bowl, pour over hot water and set aside to soak for 15 minutes.

2   Sift together wholemeal flour, self-raising flour and baking powder and return husks to bowl. Add bran cereal and mix to combine. Stir in eggs, yogurt, honey, allspice and apricot mixture and mix well.

3   Spoon batter into an 11 x 21 cm/ 4¹/₂ x 8¹/₂ in loaf tin lined with nonstick baking paper and bake for 45 minutes or until cooked when tested with a skewer.

600 kilojoules (145 Calories) per slice
Carbohydrate	29 g (80%)	very high
Fat	1 g	very low

Apricot Oatmeal Cookies

Makes 36 cookies
Oven temp: 180°C, 350°F, Gas 4

1¹/₂ cups/140 g/4¹/₂ oz rolled oats
²/₃ cup/100 g/3¹/₂ oz brown sugar
¹/₂ cup/60 g/2 oz flour, sifted
1 teaspoon baking powder
30 g/1 oz chopped dried apricots
185 g/6 oz puréed banana
3 tablespoons canola margarine, melted
2 tablespoons honey
1 teaspoon vanilla essence

1   Place rolled oats, sugar, flour and baking powder in a bowl and mix to combine.

2   Add apricots, banana, margarine, honey and vanilla essence and mix well. Place tablespoons of mixture on nonstick baking trays and bake for 8-10 minutes or until cookies are golden but still soft. Place cookies on wire racks to cool.

220 kilojoules (52 Calories) per biscuit
Carbohydrate	9 g (68%)	very high
Fat	1.5 g	very low

FATTY ACIDS

Omega-3 Fatty Acids: These are found in fish, canola, linseed, soybean and walnut oil. The omega-3 found in fish oils is more potent than in vegetable oils. Omega-3 fatty acids do not affect blood cholesterol levels, but they help prevent clotting in our blood vessels.

Trans Fatty Acids: Most of the trans fatty acids in the food supply are formed when vegetable fats are hardened by the process of hydrogenation. Hydrogenation is performed to increase shelf life and make liquid oils more solid and spreadable. Research has shown that high intakes of trans fatty acids raise our levels of LDL or 'bad' cholesterol and lower our levels of HDL or 'good' cholesterol. Large population studies in the USA suggest that high intakes of trans fatty acids increase the risk for heart and vascular disease. Fortunately, the current consumption of trans fatty acids in Australia is much lower than that in the USA!

Apricot Bran Loaf, Pumpkin Fruit Cake, Apricot Oatmeal Cookies

Pancakes

Makes 12 pancakes
Serves 6

1½ cups/185 g/6 oz self-raising flour
½ teaspoon baking powder
⅓ cup/75 g/2½ oz caster sugar
2 eggs lightly beaten
1½ cups/375 mL/12 fl oz reduced-fat milk
or buttermilk

1   Sift together flour and baking
powder into a bowl, add sugar and
mix to combine. Add eggs and milk
and mix until smooth.

2   Heat a nonstick frying pan over a
medium heat, pour 3 tablespoons of
batter into pan and cook for
1 minute each side or until golden.
Remove pancake, set aside and
keep warm. Repeat with remaining
batter. Serve pancakes hot with
honey or maple syrup.

990 kilojoules (235 Calories) per serve

Carbohydrate	45 g (75%)	very high
Fat	3 g	very low

Strawberry Sponge

Serves 12
Oven temp: 180°C, 350°F, Gas 4

SPONGE
3 eggs
½ cup/100 g/3½ oz caster sugar
¼ cup/30 g/1 oz cornflour
¼ cup/30 g/1 oz flour
¼ cup/30 g/1 oz self-raising flour
STRAWBERRY FILLING
250 g/8 oz strawberries, hulled and halved
200 g/6½ oz strawberry *fromage frais*
icing sugar

1   To make Sponge, place eggs in
a bowl and beat with an electric
mixer for 5 minutes or until light and
fluffy. Gradually add sugar, beating
well after each addition until mixture
is thick and creamy.

2   Sift together cornflour, flour and
self-raising flour.

3   Fold flour mixture into egg
mixture. Pour batter into two 18 cm/
7 in round cake tins lined with
nonstick baking paper and bake for
15 minutes or until cake springs
back when lightly pressed with
fingertips.

4   Turn cakes onto wire racks to
cool. Spread one cake with *fromage
frais* and top with strawberries.
Place remaining cake on top,
sprinkle with icing sugar and
decorate with extra strawberries, if
desired.

420 kilojoules (100 Calories) per slice

Carbohydrate	18.5 g (72%)	very high
Fat	1.5 g	very low

Right: Strawberry Sponge
Below: Pancakes

DIETING

ARE YOU OBSESSED?

For some people, especially women, dieting is a way of life. Gaining only a few grams can depress them for the day.

A dinner out ruins their diet routine. Food can no longer be enjoyed because for them it is surrounded by guilt. With society's pre-occupation with slimness, obsessive dieting is on the increase. Are you obsessed? See how you rate in the Diet Quiz.

Are you really overweight?

The fashionable body weight changes, along with hairstyles and the length of women's skirts. Marilyn Monroe would be considered fat by today's modelling agencies, as 1990s models are underweight by health standards. Therefore women whose weight is normal and healthy feel overweight next to today's models.

The relationship of your weight to your height is a starting point, but active people need to understand that they may be classified as overweight by a Body Mass Index (BMI) – even though they are not overfat. This is especially the case when there is a higher degree of muscular development as muscle is heavier than fat. Work out your BMI, then read on about better ways to measure fatness. To work out your BMI divide your weight in kilograms by the square of your height in metres.

$$\frac{\text{weight (kg)}}{\text{height}^2 \text{ (metres)}} = \text{BMI}$$

For example, if you weigh 70 kg and your height is 1.75 m

$$\frac{70 \text{ kg}}{1.75^2} = 22.86 \text{ BMI}$$

BMI
less than 20   – underweight
20-25   – healthy weight
25-30   – overweight
greater than 30   – obese

Shaping Up

Many people have a love-hate relationship with their bathroom scales. They may hate weighing themselves, but they can't resist the temptation to step on those scales.

Scales are a poor indicator of fatness for active people. Weight fluctuations can be related to changes in muscle, water or glycogen, but unfortunately we are conditioned to believe they are always fat related.

Better ways to assess fatness include:

The pinch test (skinfold measurements): Fat is pinched with skinfold callipers on various areas of the body to determine the level of body fat. This method is most useful if a skilled person takes a series of measurements over time to track progress.

Circumference measures: If you are a little too overweight for callipers, circumference measurements of your waist, hips, thighs and other parts of your body can be a better indicator of fat loss than the scales, especially if you are exercising and increasing your muscle weight.

ENERGY

All kilojoules (calories) are not equal. Protein, fat, carbo-hydrate and alcohol are the nutrients which provide energy (kilojoules/calories). Fat (37 kJ or 9 Cal/g) and alcohol (29 kJ or 7 Cal/g) provide more kilojoules/calories per gram, than either protein or carbohydrate (16 kJ or 4 Cal/g). Fat is also more easily stored as body fat when compared with protein or carbohydrate. Recent research suggests that alcohol reduces the body's ability to burn up excess fat after a fatty meal.

DIET QUIZ

Do You?	Yes	No
1 Diet even though you don't really need to lose weight (see this page).	☐	☐
2 Feel afraid to change your daily routine because you may gain weight.	☐	☐
3 Get comments from friends and family about how little you eat.	☐	☐
4 Feel guilty when you occasionally eat high-kilojoule/calorie food.	☐	☐
5 Weigh yourself daily and plan your food intake and exercise accordingly.	☐	☐
6 Count up every kilojoule (calorie) you eat.	☐	☐
7 Avoid social occasions based around food.	☐	☐
8 Worry about weight gain if you miss an exercise session.	☐	☐

Scoring: If you answer YES to most of these questions, dieting may be your obsession. Read on to find out more about the down side of dieting.

Body fat – how low can you go?

Elite athletes strive to obtain low body-fat levels for competitive reasons. While the performance benefits cannot be denied for sports such as triathlon, swimming and marathon running, sometimes athletes become obsessed with a particular fat level where even a few extra millimetres seem devastating.

Low body-fat levels may be a breeze for some, yet others struggle to get anywhere near the 'ideal' level touted by the coach, team-mates or self-taught 'experts'. Our body type is genetically determined, so there are limits to our capacity for leanness.

When an athlete's physique is not suited to a particular sport, coaches, parents and, ultimately, the athlete, need to make mature, informed and responsible decisions about methods used to manage physique-related problems. The aftermath of numerous failed dieting attempts can be devastating to both physical and mental health. If sensible approaches are unsuccessful, selecting a sport more suited to the athlete's natural physique characteristics will enable them to compete safely and develop to their full potential. Athletes such as gymnasts, ballet dancers and figure skaters, who need to be careful with their weight and food intake over a prolonged period, may benefit from a daily multi-vitamin supplement as an extra assurance that they obtain an adequate vitamin and mineral intake. Supplements however do not replace the need for a well-balanced diet.

The Yo-Yo Syndrome

Rapid and frequent weight loss and regain, known as the Yo-Yo Syndrome, is a common experience for dieters. Experts suspect that these constant weight fluctuations are the cause of longer term weight-control difficulties.
Crash weight loss reduces muscle. Weight regain is mostly fat. Little by little, with each weight-loss cycle, muscle mass is eroded away while fat mass grows with each weight regain. With less muscle, metabolism is slower. Yo-Yo dieters, systematically use dieting to slow metabolism and make it easier for their bodies to get fatter. A sensible diet and exercise plan is their only rescue. Regular exercise helps to burn up excess fat and rebuild muscle. A sensible diet provides enough fuel for the body to maintain metabolism and for it to exercise energetically, so that dieters can get off this weight-loss roller coaster for good.

Diet check: Put your favourite weight-loss diet to the test. Use the quiz on page 4 to test how balanced the diet is. The results may surprise you.

Cellulite

Cellulite is just fat – not a build-up of 'toxic waste' as you may have been led to believe. The dimply appearance is due to the fat being deposited in the leg and buttock area where connective tissue is laid down between the pockets of fat. As women have thinner skin and tend to lay down fat in this area more than men, they are more likely to have cellulite.

Excess fat in the thigh/buttock area may be unfashionable, but it has a relatively low health risk – unlike excess fat on the belly which increases the risk for heart disease, diabetes and high blood pressure. Loss of leg/buttock fat is more difficult, however, as the fat cells are more resistant. In women, the body is thought to be protective of this fat as it is used as an energy reserve to support pregnancy and breast-feeding, should that occur.

The way to lose cellulite is the same as losing fat anywhere else – sensible eating and regular aerobic exercise. Toning exercises will not help to burn fat, but will help to firm up the leg muscles to improve the overall shape.

DID YOU KNOW?

Your resting metabolic rate – the amount of fuel your body uses up at rest – is related to the amount of muscle you have. The greater the amount of muscle, the faster the metabolic rate. Fad diets lower muscle mass and your metabolism. Read the Yo-Yo Syndrome to see how incorrect dieting can actually make you fatter!

ON THE ROAD
EATING AWAY FROM HOME

One of the fringe benefits of sport is that it may open up opportunities to travel. You might start off at the next suburb but, if you get lucky, you could be off to distant, interesting places.

Food won't be the same as it is at home, so some knowledge of the typical foods eaten, the food arrangements (especially if travelling in a team), cooking facilities and the like will help you to maintain your dietary goals while you are away.

Be Prepared

The following list of questions should help you to obtain the sort of information you need to know:

1 Will food be provided or will I need to buy my own? (Important to know for your travel budget.)

2 If food is provided, what will it be? Can I buy some extras if I need to?

3 What are the best high-carbohydrate options and what high-fat dishes should I avoid ?

4 Will special airline meals be organised? If not, organise one for yourself – ask for a low-fat or vegetarian meal if special meals for athletes are not available. Stay well hydrated, drink plenty of water and avoid alcoholic or caffeine-containing drinks.

5 Is the water safe to drink? If not, drink boiled or bottled water and avoid ice, raw vegetables (washed in water) and edible skin on fruit. Avoid food at street stalls – choose reputable restaurants instead. Check if dairy products are pasteurised.

Food poisoning can really wipe out your chances of success. If you are in doubt – get some advice from a sports dietitian who can help you to plan your nutrition strategies for travelling and competition.

As you have less control over your food, it's a good idea to take a multi-vitamin supplement each day to ensure that your vitamin and mineral intake is adequate while you're away. Take your favourite sports drinks with you, as they may not be available overseas.

At the Event

Sporting venues have food outlets designed to feed spectators, not athletes. If you are going to eat well you will need to take your own food. See the section on snacks (page 11) and eating between events (page 68) for more ideas. Sports drinks are a good item to keep in your sports bag, as are non-perishable items such as breakfast cereal, instant noodles, dried fruit, water crackers, canned fruit, fruit juice and sports drinks.

Hint for Coaches

For large groups, call a local restaurant ahead of time and organise a healthy meal for when the team is due to arrive. This will speed up service and will ensure your athletes eat well. The fact that you bothered indicates to your athletes that you take seriously the need to eat well.

SUPPLEMENTS
A CONTINUING CONTROVERSY

In the pursuit of the ultimate sports performance, nutrition supplements may be used because they are believed to provide the nutritonal edge. But what do we really know about them? Here is the lowdown on just a few.

Bee Pollen

Proposed use: To provide essential vitamins and minerals which enhance athletic ability.
Scientific research: Shows it contains some essential nutrients but in quantities too small to be significant. Scientific trials have failed to demonstrate benefits to athletic performance.

Carnitine

Proposed use: To assist the transport of fatty acids into the parts of cells which handle energy production.
Claimed to assist fat burning and decrease the production of lactic acid. Also claimed to spare muscle glycogen by increasing the use of fat as a fuel – aimed at delaying fatigue in endurance events.
Scientific research: Earlier studies have shown conflicting results, but more recent studies show no benefit of supplementation on athletic performance.

Co-enzyme Q10

Proposed use: To assist with aerobic metabolism.
Scientific research: Well-designed scientific studies have demonstrated no beneficial effects from Co-enzyme Q10 supplementation in athletes.

Inosine

Proposed use: To assist endurance performance by enhancing energy production. Also to facilitate oxygen release to the muscles via its effect on red blood cell biochemistry.
Scientific research: Limited research does not support claims.

Ginseng

Proposed use: There are numerous claims regarding its potential benefits to performance and general health.
Scientific research: There has been little well-controlled research for ginseng. Studies have been hampered by a lack of consistency in the composition of different ginseng supplements.

The scientific evidence to date fails to support a performance benefit from supplementation.

Caffeine

Proposed use: To enhance endurance via its ability to increase the release of free fatty acids with sparing of muscle glycogen. Also claimed to be a psychological stimulant – used for mental arousal.
Scientific research: Research in the endurance area is conflicting and to date there is no real consensus of opinion as to whether caffeine benefits performance.

Performance benefits related to the stimulant effects seem to be dependent on the individual.

On the down side are the diuretic (dehydrating) properties of caffeine and the possible uncomfortable/ jittery response some people may experience after taking caffeine.

Athletes need to remember that caffeine is a substance which is subject to drug testing. You would need to drink 6-8 cups of coffee or 10 cans of cola drink to exceed the legal limit.

Vitamins and Minerals

Vitamins and minerals are the most popular supplements of all.

Scientific research does not support their use to enhance performance in well-nourished athletes. However, a case can be made for the use of vitamin/mineral supplements in the following situations.
Travelling: It may be difficult to keep to your optimal diet while travelling. A multi-vitamin/mineral supplement will help fill in the missing gaps. Be careful not to use travelling as an excuse to be slack with your diet.
Low energy (kilojoule/calorie) intake: For athletes such as gymnasts, figure skaters and dancers who need to keep slim or for those who are dieting to lose weight, a multi-vitamin/mineral supplement is an added assurance that they obtain the full range of vitamins and minerals on a daily basis.
Iron deficiency (diagnosed by a blood test): Supplements of iron, perhaps in conjunction with vitamin C, will be useful (see page 41).
Inadequate calcium intake: Calcium supplements may be necessary for a person who fails to meet their daily calcium requirements. They should of course make their very best effort with calcium-rich foods.

PLACEBO EFFECT

A placebo is a substance which performs no physiological function but which may benefit the taker psychologically. In other words, if you think or believe that something might help you then it's highly likely that it will.

Nutrition supplements can have a powerful psychological effect. This is one of the main reasons why so many supplements with no proven benefits remain popular. Unfortunately, many studies investigating the benefits of supplements have not taken the placebo effect into account. In these studies the true response due to the supplements is impossible to determine. A large proportion of studies investigating nutrition supplements have been poorly designed, making any conclusions from them meaningless.

Testimonials made by athletes are bound to contain an element of the placebo effect. Often these testimonials are the only support the supplement has to stand on. Clearly, there is a need for well-designed, scientific research in this area which would provide us with information about supplements that we can use with greater confidence.

CASE STUDY 1

FOOTBALL – BULKING UP

Steve

Steve is an 18-year-old Australian Rules football player who has just been drafted to a professional club. As Steve is tall and very thin, it was not long before the team gave him the nickname 'stork'.

During the first few weeks of training, Steve showed potential, but the training was tough and he soon began to feel tired and lethargic. He had also lost weight and was looking even thinner. Steve's coach pulled him aside one night and recommended he talk to the club's sports dietitian to get some help with his diet. Steve did not really like the idea of 'going on a diet' but, if it could help him gain weight and feel stronger he was prepared to give it a try.

At their first meeting the dietitian measured Steve's weight, height, body fat and took circumference measurements of his arms, legs and chest. These measurements indicated he needed to boost muscle mass, and to his surprise drop a little body fat. The dietitian asked Steve to record everything he ate and drank for one week and then hand this in for dietary analysis.

The dietary analysis showed that Steve's diet was in bad shape. Together, Steve and the dietitian worked on a list of dietary goals to help him eat better.

Steve's Dietary Goals

1   Eat larger meals and snacks – to boost energy levels and help him to gain muscle mass (see page 26).

2   Eat more carbohydrate – for energy and recovery (see page 16).

3   Eat less fat – to help lower body fat and make more room for carbohydrate foods in his diet (see page 56).

4   Balance protein – obtain adequate protein through diet (see page 27).

The dietitian worked with Steve on a new meal plan that would not only boost his energy and sports performance, but would also be enjoyable. To Steve's surprise, his eating plan was not like a diet at all. To assist with shopping and cooking, the dietitian took Steve and his flatmates (also with the team) on a shopping trip and organised a series of cooking classes with the club's home economist. They were all cooking up a storm in no time.

Steve's Statistics

Position: Full forward

Height: 182 cm

Weight: 72 kg

Sum of 8 skinfolds: 80 mm (goal less than 60 mm)

Steve's Weekly Pre-Season Training

Morning weight training: 2-3 sessions each of 1-1½ hours

Afternoon football/fitness sessions: 4 sessions each of 2-2½ hours

Steve's Food Record

BREAKFAST
2 cups Cornflakes
1 cup milk
1 cup tea with 1 teaspoon sugar

SNACK
1 chocolate bar or bag of chips
1 can soft drink

LUNCH
1 pie or a ham or schnitzel sandwich
1 pack potato crisps or a piece of cake
1 can soft drink

SNACK (BEFORE TRAINING)
Mostly nothing or sometimes a banana
Sports drink after training

DINNER
Fast food most nights.
Steve's favourite is ½ supreme pizza reheated from the freezer. Occasionally, a grilled T-bone steak, oven bake chips and a bread roll.

BEFORE BED
Two amino acid capsules

FRIDAY AND SATURDAY NIGHT
Quite a few beers and a couple of hot dogs outside the night club on the way home

Dietary Analysis (Typical Daily Analysis)
Energy: 9,525 kilojoules (2,270 Calories)
Protein: 80 g (14%)
Fat: 97 g (39%)
Carbohydrate: 273 g (47%)

Steve's New Meal Plan

BREAKFAST
1 piece of fruit
2 cups/125 g/4 oz wholegrain cereal
2 cups/500 mL/16 fl oz reduced-fat milk
2 slices wholegrain or white toast with a scrape of butter or margarine and some jam or honey
1 glass /250 mL/8 fl oz fruit juice

SNACK
1 sandwich or a piece fruit and a low-fat yogurt or 1 muffin (page 11)
1 carton (250 mL/8 fl oz) fruit juice

LUNCH
3 salad sandwiches or rolls with lean meat, chicken, reduced-fat cheese, egg, canned tuna in springwater or canned salmon
2 pieces fruit
600 mL/1 pt flavoured reduced-fat milk

SNACK (1-2 hours before training)
2 pieces fruit and 500 mL/16 fl oz of milk-based smoothie such as the ones on page 31 or a commercial liquid meal

SNACK (after training)
After training, 1 litre/1¾ pt sports drink

DINNER
Large serving lean meat (155 g/5 oz), skinless chicken (185 g/6 oz) or fish (250 g/8 oz) – grilled or cooked with minimal oil
Large serving cooked rice, pasta or potato
Medium serving vegetables or tossed green salad (no-oil dressing)
4 slices bread or 2 bread rolls (no butter or margarine)
2 pieces fresh fruit or a dessert from the weekly meal plan

SUPPER
Choose a snack from Sporting Snacks (page 11)
500 mL/16 fl oz milk-based smoothie (page 31) or a commercial liquid meal

FRIDAY AND SATURDAY NIGHT
Eat a meal before going out and reduce alcohol intake. Keep the heavier drinking sessions for special occasions only.

Dietary Analysis of New Meal Plan
Energy: 18,821 kilojoules (4,480 Calories)
Protein: 194 g (17%)
Fat: 67 g (14%)
Carbohydrate: 775 g (69%)

Typical Weekly Menu

The dietitian outlined a weekly plan of dinner recipes for the household. Once Steve and his flatmates could master this group of recipes, the dietitian suggested that they try other high carbohydrate recipes from this book. Steve would need to eat the equivalent of 2 serves from the recipes in this book.

MONDAY
Mongolian Lamb (page 62) served with rice or noodles (as in the recipe) and steamed vegetables
4 slices bread or 2 bread rolls
1 Banana Muffin (page 11)

TUESDAY
Pitta Pizzas (page 60) served with a tossed green salad (no-oil dressing)
4 slices bread or 2 bread rolls
Fruit salad and lite ice-cream

WEDNESDAY
Chilli Chicken Stir-Fry (page 42) served with pasta (as in the recipe), rice or noodles and extra steamed vegetables
4 slices bread or 2 bread rolls
2 Apple Toast Turnovers (page 14)

THURSDAY
1 Steak Sandwich (page 64) served with a tossed green salad (no-oil dressing)
Perfect Potato Salad (page 25)
2 slices bread or 1 bread roll
2 Pancakes (page 76)

FRIDAY
Pasta with Mushroom and Ham Sauce (page 38) served with a tossed green salad (no-oil dressing) or steamed vegetables
4 slices bread or 2 bread rolls
2 pieces fresh fruit

SATURDAY
Sweet and Sour Chicken (page 58) served with rice (as in the recipe) or noodles and extra steamed vegetables
4 slices bread or 2 bread rolls
2 Chocolate Brownies (page 70)

SUNDAY
Lite Lasagne (page 44) served with steamed vegetables or a tossed green salad (no-oil dressing)
4 slices bread or 2 bread rolls
2 Pancakes (page 76)

RESULTS

Steve went on to lose body fat and gain 3.5 kg/7 lbs of weight in the pre-season. He gained a further 2 kg/4 lb over the year. He even had his first run in senior grade.

CASE STUDY 2
GYMNASTICS – DIETING BLUES

Dianna

Dianna is a 14-year-old gymnast who has her heart set on representing her country in gymnastics. Her biggest problem is her weight. Although she has tried a number of diets, she finds that she 'just can't keep to a diet'. During the morning it is easy, but in the afternoon and evening she gets hungry and craves snack foods, especially chocolate. Dianna always feels tired when dieting and often can't concentrate at school.

Dianna has a love-hate relationship with the scales; she weighs herself at least once a day. When her weight is up, she feels depressed and then it is even more difficult for her to stay on a diet. Dianna's gymnastic coach could sense that she was having difficultly coping with her weight so suggested that she see a sports dietitian for some help with her tiredness and dieting problem.

At their first meeting, the dietitian took a history of Dianna's weight and eating patterns. It was obvious from this history that Dianna was not eating enough through the day, and then getting hungry in the afternoon and evening. The dietitian explained that dieting can slow metabolism and gave Dianna some information to read (see page 78).

The first strategy for Dianna was to eat more breakfast and lunch and stop weighing herself every day. The dietitian also asked Dianna to keep a record of her food intake and rate her hunger before each meal. A visit to her doctor to have her iron status checked was also recommended.

To her surprise, Dianna felt much better eating more breakfast and lunch. She also felt less hungry in the afternoon and evening and was more in control of her food intake. It was actually easier to forget about chocolate!

At their next session, the dietitian measured Dianna's body fat. Both Dianna and the dietitian agreed that it would be better if body fat measurements were used to assess her progress rather than the scales, especially until Dianna felt more confident about losing fat. As the dietitian had suspected, Dianna's iron test results indicated that she was iron deficient. This explained why she was feeling so tired. Dianna's doctor recommended she take some iron supplements for a short time and also suggested she increase the iron in her diet.

The dietitian made some adjustments to Dianna's meal plan which included more iron rich foods. The importance of vitamin C rich fruits and vegetables for boosting iron absorption was highlighted and the problem of excess tannin and caffeine was also discussed (see page 41). As chocolate was still a favourite food, the dietitian stressed the importance of including chocolate in the diet occasionally as a treat. Recipes for lower fat chocolate flavoured alternatives were given. The Chocolate Brownies (page 70) became one of Dianna's favourites.

Dianna's Diet History

BREAKFAST
1 slice wholegrain toast with butter
1 cup black coffee

SNACK
2 crispbreads with butter
1 cup black coffee

LUNCH
Green salad
Apple
1 cup black coffee

SNACK
Chocolate or chocolate biscuits
1 can diet cola

DINNER
Steamed vegetables
Sometimes steamed chicken
1 cup black coffee

SUPPER
Chocolate or chocolate biscuits
1 cup black coffee

DIETARY ANALYSIS (DAILY INTAKE)
Energy:	*7,050 kilojoules (1,680 Calories)*
Protein:	*53 g (13%)*
Fat:	*79 g (42%)*
Carbohydrate:	*198 g (45%)*
Calcium:	*637 mg (recommended daily intake > 800 mg)*
Iron:	*7.9 mg (recommended daily intake 12-16 mg)*

Dianna's Weekly Training Program

Gymnastics training 6 mornings and 5 evenings per week each session 2-3 hours.

Dianna's New Meal Plan

BREAKFAST
1 piece fruit
1 cup/60 g/2 oz wholegrain cereal with reduced-fat milk
1 slice wholegrain toast with a scrape of butter and jam
1 cup/250 mL/8 fl oz decaffeinated coffee

SNACK
1 piece of fruit or 200 g/6½ oz carton of reduced-fat yogurt or a Chocolate Brownie (page 70) or 1 slice raisin toast with a scrape of butter or margarine
Water, herbal tea or decaffeinated coffee

LUNCH
Salad sandwich on wholegrain bread with minimal butter or margarine
Protein options for the sandwich include: Chicken, turkey, canned tuna in springwater, canned salmon, egg, lean ham, lean roast or corned beef or reduced-fat cheese
1 piece fruit
Water or a diet drink (not containing caffeine)

SNACK
Same options as for morning snack

DINNER
Small serving lean meat (90 g/3 oz), skinless chicken (125 g/4 oz) or fish (155 g/5 oz) – grilled or cooked with minimal or no oil
2 potatoes or 1 cup/185 g/6 oz cooked rice or a bowl cooked pasta
Large serve steamed vegetables or a salad with low-oil dressing
Water or diet cordial

SUPPER
1 glass /250 mL/8 fl oz reduced-fat milk
1 slice raisin toast with jam or honey
1 cup/250 mL/8 fl oz herbal tea or decaffeinated coffee

Dietary Analysis of New Meal Plan

Energy:	*5,640 kilojoules (1,300 Calories)*
Protein:	*80 g (24%)*
Fat:	*20 g (14%)*
Carbohydrate:	*208 g (62%)*
Calcium:	*800 mg*
Iron:	*14-18 mg*

Reduced-Fat Iron-Rich Dinners

The following are examples of tasty reduced-fat, iron-rich dinners which Dianna now enjoys. Dianna's serving size is a little smaller than indicated in the recipes in this book.

Mongolian Lamb (page 62) served with rice or noodles (as in the recipe) and steamed vegetables or a salad (low-oil dressing)

Sesame Beef (page 62) served with rice or noodles (as in the recipe)

Curry Lamb Stir-Fry (page 43) served with rice (as in the recipe)

Thai Beef (page 42) served with rice (as in the recipe) or noodles and steamed vegetables or tossed green salad (low-oil dressing)

Lean Roast (page 40) served with roast vegetables (as in the recipe) and steamed green vegetables

Beef Skewers (page 36) served with rice (as in the recipe) and a tossed green salad (low-oil dressing) or steamed vegetables

Results

Dianna lost fat and felt more energetic in school and training. This was the first kind of diet she could really keep to, mainly because it was not really like a diet. Giving up crash dieting was Dianna's secret to success.

CASE STUDY 3

TRIATHLON – SLAVE TO DIET

Tom

Tom is a 24-year-old computer programmer and keen triathlete. Over the past 4 years Tom has competed in Olympic distance triathlons but his dream has always been to compete in the Hawaii Iron Man. To achieve this, Tom knew he had to train much harder, improve his diet and lose that extra bit of body fat he was carrying.

Tom started increasing his training gradually. Initially he felt great, and was especially happy with the loss of body fat. The increased carbohydrate intake from his now very low-fat diet was boosting his energy levels. However, as the months went on Tom's performance and health started to deteriorate. At first Tom thought he had a virus, but several trips to the doctor failed to find evidence of infection or iron deficieny.

Jenny, Tom's wife suspected his diet may be the cause of his problems. Tom was convinced his dietary intake which now eliminated all treat foods, red meat and alcohol was not to blame. Jenny had noticed Tom was more moody lately and she suspected he had lost too much weight. Tom had certainly become a hermit. He never went out to eat – just in case the food had too much oil in it.

Tom's doctor recommended he see a sports dietitian. To his surprise, the dietitian confirmed he had become a 'slave to diet' and obsessive about food. The dietitian found that his energy and protein intake were too low. Although most of his kilojoules (calories) came from carbohydrates, he was not eating enough food to fuel his body for training. The dietitian advised Tom on how to recover faster by including adequate carbohydrate

and fluid after each training session (see pages 19 and 32)

It took a little while for Tom to feel comfortable eating more protein foods. After all, he knew that even lean meat, chicken and fish contained some fat. However, he had to admit he did feel much better. Jenny noticed he was not so moody and that his muscle tone was returning.

The dietitian monitored Tom's body fat to reassure him the dietary changes would still allow him to maintain a low body-fat level. After a few months Tom regained enough confidence to take Jenny out for dinner, including a glass of wine and some dessert. He realised that food was more than just fuel, it was an enjoyable aspect of his life he had forgotten about.

Tom's Statistics

Height: 178 cm
Weight: 63 kg
Sum of 8 skinfolds: 45 mm

Tom's Weekly Training Program

Run: 60 km
Swim: 15 km
Cycle: 400 km

Tom's Diet History

BREAKFAST
2 cups bran cereal
1 cup skim milk
1 banana
1 cup herbal tea

SNACK
4 rice cakes with honey (no butter or margarine)

LUNCH
2 salad sandwiches on wholegrain bread (no butter or margarine)
2 pieces of fruit
Bottled water

SNACK
4 rice cakes with honey (no butter or margarine)

DINNER
1 cup dried beans
Large plate steamed rice or pasta
Large quantity of steamed vegetables
Fresh fruit salad

SUPPER
1 banana

Dietary Analysis (Typical Intake)
Energy:	*8,802 kilojoules (2,095 Calories)*
Protein:	*84 g (17%)*
Fat:	*14 g (6%)*
Carbohydrate:	*410g (77%)*

Tom's New Meal Plan

BREAKFAST
1-2 pieces fresh fruit
2 cups/125 g/4 oz wholegrain cereal (change the type regularly) with skim or reduced-fat milk
3 slices toast with jam, honey or marmalade
2 glasses/500 mL/16 fl oz fruit juice

SNACK
1 banana and honey roll and a low-fat yogurt or lean meat or chicken sandwich
1 glass/250 mL/8 fl oz fruit juice or
1-2 snacks from Sporting Snacks (page 11)

LUNCH
3 salad sandwiches with lean protein fillings such as chicken, canned tuna in springwater, canned salmon, egg, lean ham or corned beef or reduced-fat cheese
1 piece fresh fruit
1 snack from Sporting Snacks (page 11)
1 glass/250 mL/8 fl oz fruit juice

SNACK (1-2 hours before training)
As for morning tea or if training some fruit and a sports drink or a fruit smoothie (page 31)

DINNER
Medium serving lean meat (125 g/4 oz), skinless chicken (155 g/5 oz), fish (200 g/6½ oz) or a vegetarian meal.
Large serving rice, pasta or potato
Medium serving vegetables or tossed green salad with no-oil dressing
4 slices bread or 2 bread rolls
2 pieces fresh fruit or a dessert from the meal plan
1 glass/250 mL/8 fl oz fruit juice

SUPPER
As for morning snack

Dietary Analysis of New Meal Plan
Energy:	*18,925 kilojoules (4,500 Calories)*
Protein:	*195 g (17%)*
Fat:	*85 g (16%)*
Carbohydrate:	*744 g (67%)*

Typical Weekly Menu

The dietitian outlined a weekly plan for Tom to follow initially. Once he felt more confident eating different types of protein he was encouraged to use other recipe ideas.

MONDAY
Spicy Stir-Fried Noodles (page 52) served with extra steamed vegetables
4 slices bread or 2 bread rolls
2 pieces fresh fruit
1 glass/250 mL/8 fl oz fruit juice

TUESDAY
Penne with Pumpkin Sauce (page 51) served with a tossed green salad (no-oil dressing) or steamed vegetables
4 slices bread or 2 bread rolls
1 serving Quick Fruit Bread Pudding (page 72)
1 glass/250 mL/8 fl oz fruit juice

WEDNESDAY
Speedy Paella (page 46) served with tossed green salad (no-oil dressing)
4 slices bread or 2 bread rolls
Canned fruit and lite ice-cream
1 glass/250 mL/8 fl oz fruit juice

THURSDAY
Lite Lasagne (page 44) served with tossed green salad (no-oil dressing) or steamed green vegetables
4 slices bread or 2 bread rolls
2 Apple Toast Turnovers (page 14) with lite *fromage frais*
1 glass/250 mL/8 fl oz fruit juice

FRIDAY
Cajun Fish and Chips (page 48) served with steamed green vegetables or tossed green salad (no-oil dressing)
4 slices bread or 2 bread rolls
Fresh fruit salad
1 glass/250 mL/8 fl oz fruit juice

SATURDAY
Thai Beef (page 42) served with extra steamed green vegetables or a tossed green salad (no-oil dressing)
4 slices bread or 2 bread rolls
1 serving Mango Cheesecake (page 73)
1 glass/250 mL/8 fl oz fruit juice

SUNDAY
Chicken Pizza (page 60) served with a tossed green salad (no-oil dressing)
4 slices bread or 2 bread rolls
1 Fruit Smoothie (page 31)
1 glass/250 mL/8 fl oz fruit juice

Results

Tom went on to qualify for and give his best ever performance in the Hawaii Iron Man later in the year. Tom realised that he could perform better as a triathlete by balancing his diet rather than being a slave to it.

CASE STUDY 4
SWIMMING – REFUELLING BETWEEN EVENTS

Nick

Nick is a 14-year-old swimmer who is training for the National championships to be held next month. Nick has been swimming extremely well in training lately and if he can do his personal best times at the championships, he should be able to win a few medals, perhaps even a gold. One of the major problems for Nick is keeping his energy levels up over the day. When he feels nervous he finds it difficult to eat. As a result, he usually feels tired by the evening when he has to pull out his best performance for the finals.

Nick hates having anything heavy in his stomach during the day so he doesn't usually eat, but does try to drink water to replace his fluids. Looking for the nutritional edge, Nick consulted a sports dietitian for assistance with his competition eating plan.

The dietitian took a history of Nick's training diet and was impressed that he was really following a well balanced, high carbohydrate eating plan. The dietitian explained that Nick would need to make sure he ate similarly in the weeks leading up to the National championships, but as he would be tapering his training he may not feel as hungry. Although it was fine to cut back on the food intake a little during this time, he should still maintain a high carbohydrate intake.

Nick usually felt too nervous to eat breakfast on the morning of the meet. The dietitian reassured Nick that he did not have to eat a lot for breakfast then, but it was important to eat some carbohydrate to top up his glycogen stores, especially in the liver (see page 68). Together they discussed liquid meals which have the advantage of being high in energy and low in bulk – perfect for nervous stomachs! Nick decided to try a homemade fruit smoothie (see page 31 for ideas) and a commercial liquid meal before one of his club races on Friday night to determine which meal he liked best. He thought the suggestion of topping up his carbohydrate stores with sports drink (page 68) and a little food during the day was a great idea.

The dietitian also gave him some food ideas to practise with at his Friday night club meets. Nick could experiment with different foods and work out which ones worked best for him. As a general rule he would use sports drink when there was less than 1 hour between races. In longer breaks he could try a small portion of the foods listed as suitable to try between events (page 89) with some sports drink or water to top up his fluids.

Nick's Training Diet

PRE-MORNING TRAINING
Sports (fluid replacement) drink
1 banana

BREAKFAST
2 glasses/500 mL/16 fl oz fruit juice
2 bananas
2 cups/125 g/4 oz wholegrain cereal with skim or reduced-fat milk
2 slices mixed grain toast with honey or jam (no butter or margarine)

RECESS AT SCHOOL
1 glass/250 mL/8 fl oz fruit juice
2 pieces fresh fruit with 200 g/6½ oz reduced-fat yogurt or 1 sandwich with lean meat or salad (no butter or margarine) or 1 fruit muffin and 1 piece fresh fruit

LUNCH AT SCHOOL
3 sandwiches or bread rolls with either lean meat, chicken, cheese, canned tuna in springwater, canned salmon, egg or salad (use reduced-fat mayonnaise instead of butter or margarine)
1 carton/250 m/8 fl oz fruit juice

SNACK AFTER SCHOOL (pre-training)
Sports (fluid replacement) drink
1 banana

AFTER TRAINING
Sports (fluid replacement) drink

DINNER
Large serving lean meat (155 g/ 5 oz) – usually 3-4 times a week – skinless chicken (185 g/6 oz) or fish (250 g/8 oz) – cooked in a reduced-fat way
Large serving rice, pasta or potato
Medium serving vegetables or tossed green salad with no-oil dressing
2 slices bread lightly spread with butter or margarine
2 pieces fresh fruit or occasionally a dessert

SUPPER
Fruit smoothie

Dietary Analysis
Energy:	*16,770 kilojoules (3,995 Calories)*
Protein:	*175 g (18%)*
Fat:	*60 g (13%)*
Carbohydrate:	*688 g (69%)*

Typical program of events

8.30 am	Arrive at the pool	5.00 pm	Arrive at the pool
8.30-9.00 am	Warm up	5.00-5.30 pm	Warm up
Morning Heats		**Evening Finals**	
10.15 am	100 metre Butterfly	6.30 pm	100 metre Butterfly
11.40 am	200 metre Freestyle	8.00 pm	200 metre Freestyle
12.45 pm	100 metre Freestyle	8.45 pm	100 metre Freestyle
Break			

Suitable Foods For Between Events

Note: After eating allow at least 1 hour for digestion.
Soft fresh (preferably peeled) or canned fruit
Honey, jam or banana sandwiches
Raisin bread or fruit bun
Plain scones with jam
Jelly
Jelly beans or jelly lollies
Sports bars
Quick Banana Rice Custard (page 14)
Banana Muffins (page 11)
Muesli Bars (page 11)
Pikelets (page 14)
Pumpkin Fruit Cake (page 74)

Results

Nick won the bronze medal for the 100 metre Butterfly, swam a personal best time for the 200 metre Freestyle and won a gold in the 100 metre Freestyle. This was his best ever performance. Fine-tuning his competition diet was an integral part in his success.

New Eating Strategy for Competition

After a couple of weeks practising with the foods above and some different sports drinks, Nick felt that he was ready to fine tune his competition eating plan. With the help of the dietitian they came up with the following strategy.

EVENING PRIOR TO THE CHAMPIONSHIPS
Nick's usual high carbohydrate meal – pasta with a lean bolognaise sauce and fresh bread and for dessert Pancakes (page 76).

PRE-COMPETITION BREAKFAST
Powershake (page 31) – made without the bran
1 Banana Muffin (page 11)

8.30 am   Arrive at the pool
8.30-9.00 am   Warm up

POST WARM UP SNACK (9.00 am)
Sports (fluid replacement) drink
1 Banana Muffin (page 11)

MORNING HEATS
10.15 am   100 metre Butterfly
11.40 am   200 metre Freestyle
12.45 pm   100 metre Freestyle

AFTER EACH RACE
Sports (fluid replacement) drink

BREAK (1.30 pm)
Sweet and Sour Chicken (page 58) served with rice
   (as in the recipe), noodles or pasta
Fruit juice
Fruit jelly

5.00 pm   Arrive at the pool
5.00-5.30 pm   Warm up

POST WARM UP SNACK (5.30 pm)
Sports (fluid replacement) drink
1 Banana Muffin (page 11)

EVENING FINALS
6.30 pm   100 metre Butterfly
8.00 pm   200 metre Freestyle
8.30 pm   100 metre Freestyle

AFTER EACH RACE
Sports (fluid replacement) drink between each race and
   between the 100 metre Butterfly and 200 metre
   Freestyle a honey sandwich on white bread

AFTER RACES
Leftover Sweet and Sour Chicken and rice, noodles or
   pasta while watching the last races.

CARBOHYDRATE AND FAT COUNTER

Food Description	Serve Size	Carbohydrate (g)	Fat (g)
BEVERAGES			
Cordial	250 mL	19	0
Cappuccino	200 mL	4.5	3.5
Coffee (white)	200 mL	1.0	1
Juice (100%)	250 mL	18.5	0
Soft drink	250 mL	27	0
Tea (white)	200 mL	1.0	1
Sport Supplements*			
Fluid Replacers	100 mL	5-10	0
Sports Meal	100 g powder	62	16
Sustagen Sport	100 g powder	64	1.3
Lucozade	100 mL	18.3	0
BISCUITS			
Chocolate-coated	1 biscuit	9	3.5
Cheese cracker	4 small	15	4
Cream biscuit	1 biscuit	10	3.5
Plain craker	1 large	4	0.8
Plain sweet biscuit	1 biscuit	5.5	1.5
Shortbread biscuit	1 biscuit	10	4.5
CAKES AND DESSERTS			
Apple pie	1 slice (135 g)	36.5	18.5
Black Forest cake	1 slice	32	35
Carrot cake	1 large slice	33	42
Cheesecake	1 slice	36	26.5
Chocolate eclair	1 individual	23	18
Chocolate mousse	1 medium	15	15
Croissant	1 large	23	16
Custard tart	1 individual	41	20
Danish pastry	1 individual	35	16
Doughnut (iced)	1 individual	38.5	20
Fruit cake	1 slice	33.5	6
Lamington	1 individual	19	6
Pancake (commercial)	1 pancake	26	12
Scone	1 scone	22	4
CEREALS			
Breads			
crumpet	1	20	0.5
English muffin	1	25.5	1
white	1 slice	14	0.8
wholegrain	1 slice	12	1
bread roll	1	24	1.5
Lebanese bread	1 large round	60	2.5
pitta bread	1 medium round	39	1.8
Breakfast Cereals			
Coco Pops	1 cup	26.5	1
Cornflakes	1 cup	25.5	0.5
Just Right	1 cup	45	1
muesli (Swiss)	1/4 cup	31.5	5.5
muesli (toasted)	1/4 cup	32	10
porridge	1 cup	33	2.5
Sultana Bran	1 cup	32	1
Sustain	1 cup	40	2.5
Weet-Bix	2 biscuits	19	1
Pasta and Rice (Boiled)			
white pasta	1 cup	36	0.5
wholemeal	1 cup	36	1
Chinese noodles	1 pack	51	0.5
white rice	1 cup	53	0.5
brown rice	1 cup	57	1.5
barley	1 cup	36	1.5

Food Description	Serve Size	Carbohydrate (g)	Fat (g)
EGGS			
Boiled (50 g)	1	0	6
Fried (50 g)	1	0	8.5
Omelette	2 eggs	0	18
Quiche	average slice	21.5	45
ETHNIC FOODS			
Chicken Chop Suey	average serve	5	10
Falafel	1 small	4.5	4.5
Lasagne	average serve	29.5	13.5
Moussaka	average serve	24.5	25
Ravoili	average serve	36.5	13
Spaghetti Bolognese	average serve	72	18.5
Sweet and Sour Pork	average serve	44	54
FAST FOODS			
Sausage roll	1 individual	31.5	23
Meat pie	1 individual	34	24
Chicken			
nuggets	6	13.5	20
barbecue (with skin on)	breast	0	12
	leg and thigh	0	18
deep-fried	average piece	0	15
Hamburgers			
Big Mac	1	43.5	27
Cheeseburger	1	25.5	16
Pizza			
Hawaiian (thin base)	1/4 medium	34	11
Supreme (thin base)	1/4 medium	49	18.5
FATS AND OILS			
Butter	1 teaspoon	0	4
Cream			
Full cream	1 tablespoon	0	14
Light cream	1 tablespoon	0	7
Cream cheese	1 tablespoon	0	10
French dressing	1 tablespoon	0	5
Mayonnaise	1 tablespoon	4	6.5
Margarine	1 teaspoon	0	4
Oil	1 tablespoon	0	20
Sour cream	1 tablespoon	0	7.5
FISH AND SEAFOODS			
Fish Fingers			
fried	1 finger	4	4
grilled	1 finger	4	2.8
King prawns, fresh	1 prawn	0	0.5
Salmon	100 g	0	10.5
Tuna (canned)			
in brine	100 g	0	2
in oil	100 g	0	11
White fish (grilled)	150 g	0	1
White fish (fried)	150 g	0	23.5
FRUITS			
Apple	1 medium	13	0
Avocado	1/2 medium	0.5	20
Banana	1 medium	28	0
Cherries	25 medium	15	0
Coconut cream	1/2 cup	4.5	25
Grapes	20 medium	15	0
Kiwifruit	2 medium	17	0
Mandarin	2 medium	15	0
Mango	1 small	13	0
Melon/cantaloupe	1/2 small	15	0

CARBOHYDRATE AND FAT COUNTER (CONTINUED)

Food Description	Serve Size	Carbohydrate (g)	Fat (g)
FRUITS (cont.)			
Orange	1 medium	12	0
Pear	1 medium	15	0
MEATS (fresh)			
Bacon (grilled)			
with fat	1 rasher	0	7
lean	1 rasher	0	3
Beef (grilled)			
Hamburger patty	1 large patty	0	24
Round Steak			
with fat	200 g	0	33
lean	150 g	0	10
Topside Roast			
with fat	90 g	0	9
lean	80 g	0	4
Lamb (grilled)			
Chump Chop			
with fat	1 chop	0	12
lean only	1 chop	0	4.5
Trim lamb fillet	100 g	0	4
Pork (grilled)			
Pork chop			
with fat	1 chop	0	30
lean	1 chop	0	3.5
Butterfly steak	100 g	0	4.5
Veal (grilled)			
Veal chop			
with fat	1 chop	0	2.5
lean	1 chop	0	1.5
Leg steak	100 g	0	1
Schnitzel (fried)	200 g	0	28
MEATS (processed)			
Devon	2 slices	0	9
Frankfurter	1 individual	3.4	21
Ham			
leg	2 slices	0	3.5
light leg	2 slices	0	2
Salami (average fat)	3-4 small slices	0	19
Sausage (grilled)			
beef (60 g)	1	3	11
pork (60 g)	1	3.5	13
DAIRY AND SOY PRODUCTS			
Milk			
Skim	100 mL	5	0.1
2% fat	100 mL	5.5	1.5-2.5
Full-fat	100 mL	4.6	3.8
Soy	100 mL	2.5	3.2
Lite soy	100 mL	3.0	0.1
Banana Smoothie			
Skim	250 mL	40	1
Full-fat	250 mL	36	10
Cheese			
Fancy			
Camerbert	30 g	0	8
feta	30 g	0	7.5
mozzarella	30 g	0	7
Parmesan	30 g	0	10
Cheddar			
processed Cheddar	30 g	0	10

Food Description	Serve Size	Carbohydrate (g)	Fat (g)
Cheese (cont.)			
super light	30 g	0	3
Soft			
cottage (regular)	100 g	0	9.5
cottage (low-fat)	100 g	0	1
cream (regular)	30 g	0	10
cream (light)	30 g	0	5
ricotta (regular)	100 g	0	11.5
ricotta (reduced-fat)	100 g	0	4.5
POULTRY			
Chicken			
breast with skin	100 g	0	12
breast without skin	90 g	0	3.5
leg with skin	1 drumstick	0	7
leg without skin	1 drumstick	0	3.5
Turkey			
white meat	100 g	0	1.5
dark meat	100 g	0	4
NUTS			
Almonds	50 g	2.4	27
Cashews	50 g	13.2	25.5
Peanuts	50 g	7	26.5
SAUCES			
Brown gravy	1 tablespoon	1.5	1.5
Tomato sauce	1 tablespoon	6	0.5
White sauce	1 tablespoon	3	0.5
SNACK FOODS			
Chips	50 g pack	27	16
Corn Chips (CC's)	50 g pack	25.5	13.5
Chocolate			
plain	100 g	62	27.5
bar	60 g	37.5	11
Muesli Bar			
fruit (average)	1 bar	2	4.5
chocolate-coated (average)	1 bar	2	6.5
Pretzels	50 g	32.5	1.8
Twisties	50 g pack	29	13.5
VEGETABLES			
Beetroot	3 slices	7	0
Corn	1 large cob	39	1.5
Green (steamed)	1 cup	0.5	0
Potato			
boiled	1 medium	15	0
chips	1 cup	25	20
mashed	2 scoops	15	5
roasted	1 medium	15	2.5
sweet (boiled)	1/2 cup	18	0
Peas (green)	2 tablespoons	5	0
Pumpkin (steamed)	2 pieces	8	0
Legumes			
baked beans	1/2 cup	10	0
soy beans	1/2 cup	1	6.5
YOGHURT			
Fruit	200 g carton	25	4
Fruit (low-fat)	200 g carton	26	0.5

Figures used directly or in calculating values for recipes have been taken from Nutritional Values of Australian Foods (Australian Goverment Publishing Services). Some other values have been taken from published work of Assoicate Professor Heather Greenfield and Professor R.B.H. Wills at the University of NSW. * From product information.

INDEX